Powerful
PROFESSIONAL
DEVELOPMENT

To educators interested in improving schools from within by making "good" teaching, "great" teaching.

Powerful
PROFESSIONAL
DEVELOPMENT

Building Expertise
WITHIN THE
FOUR WALLS
of Your School

DIANE YENDOL-HOPPEY • NANCY FICHTMAN DANA

Foreword by Stephanie Hirsh

CORWIN
A SAGE Company

For information:

Corwin
A SAGE Company
2455 Teller Road
Thousand Oaks, California 91320
(800) 233-9936
Fax: (800) 417-2466
www.corwin.com

SAGE Ltd.
1 Oliver's Yard
55 City Road
London EC1Y 1SP
United Kingdom

SAGE India Pvt. Ltd.
B 1/I 1 Mohan Cooperative Industrial Area
Mathura Road, New Delhi 110 044
India

SAGE Asia-Pacific Pte. Ltd.
33 Pekin Street #02-01
Far East Square
Singapore 048763

Printed in the United States of America

Library of Congress Cataloging-in-Publication Data

Yendol-Hoppey, Diane.
Powerful professional development: building expertise within the four walls of your school/ Diane Yendol-Hoppey and Nancy Fichtman Dana; foreword by Stephanie Hirsh.
 p. cm.
Includes bibliographical references and index.
ISBN 978-1-4129-7975-7 (pbk.)
 1. Teachers—In-service training. 2. Professional learning communities. I. Dana, Nancy Fichtman, 1964– II. Title.

LB1731.Y375 2010
370.71′55—dc22   2009051389

This book is printed on acid-free paper.

10 11 12 13 14 10 9 8 7 6 5 4 3 2 1

Acquisitions Editor:	Carol Chambers Collins
Associate Editor:	Julie McNall
Editorial Assistants:	Brett Ory and Allison Scott
Production Editor:	Jane Haenel
Copy Editor:	Adam Dunham
Typesetter:	C&M Digitals (P) Ltd.
Proofreader:	Ellen Howard
Indexer:	Molly Hall
Cover and Graphic Designer:	Scott Van Atta

Contents

Foreword

I t was my first year as a district staff developer, and I was so excited—and so unprepared!—to plan my first staff development experience for the school principals. At the conclusion of the evening, I collected evaluation forms from the few who remained until the bitter end; as you might imagine, the ratings were poor. I'll never forget the following comment: "Who hired this person, and what makes her think she knows what would be helpful to principals?"

After working through the shock of the experience, I vowed I would spend the next several years proving I was the right choice. More importantly, I set out to ensure that whatever the district offered in the future for principals would meet their needs and, someday, exceed their expectations. I had a lot to learn.

In the 1980s, many educators across the country, not just in my school system, described their professional development experiences as large-group lectures delivered by so-called experts who someone else had determined would be helpful to them in their classrooms. They resented the fact that, like the principals in my district, they were asked neither what help they needed nor how they would prefer to use their staff development time. Fortunately, there were many educators who recognized that there had to be better ways to plan professional development and some who spoke and wrote specifically on that subject to help us.

In 1990 Dennis Sparks and Susan Loucks-Horsley introduced a new framework for professional development in "Five Models of Teacher Development." They described meaningful, engaging approaches to professional development—including action research, study groups, peer observation, lesson planning with colleagues, and journal writing—that were very different from what most educators were experiencing. And staff developers across the country saw the framework as offering a new way to think about organizing their work.

Then in 1994 Dennis Sparks wrote an article, "A Paradigm Shift in Staff Development," in which he stated, "History teaches us the power of a transforming idea, an alteration in world view so profound that all that

follows is changed forever. Such a paradigm shift is now rapidly transforming the discipline of 'staff development.'" Sparks described three
powerful ideas he viewed as shaping schools in the United States: results-
driven education, systems thinking, and constructivism. In response to
these shifts, he said that staff development must change as well. In 1997
Dennis Sparks and I coauthored *A New Vision for Staff Development* and presented eleven shifts we observed taking place, offering case studies from
the field as our evidence. One of those shifts is the subject of this book: the
movement from training conducted away from the job as the primary
delivery system for staff development to multiple forms of job-embedded
learning.

Educators advocating for job-embedded learning were confident that
it would be more helpful than the typical professional development most
teachers were still experiencing. Job-embedded learning was based on the
assumption that "the most powerful learning is that which occurs in
response to challenges currently being faced by the learner and that allows
for immediate application, experimentation, and adaptation on the job"
(Sparks & Hirsh, 1997, p. 52). While many educators reported that they
wanted to move away from the more traditional staff development, there
were few examples or reasons to assist organizations interested in making
the shift.

Then the standards and accountability era began, and school performance ratings became public. Research confirmed that teachers were the
single most important factor influencing student learning, which meant
school systems had to find ways to improve the quality of teaching if all
students were to successfully achieve new standards. Savvy district and
school leaders recognized professional development as the key and also
realized that one-size-fits-all workshops would not meet the needs of a
diverse teaching staff. These educators knew that the most powerful learning occurs closest to the work of the learner, when learners (in this case,
teachers) are able to see an immediate impact from the results of their
efforts. And confining professional development to two days a year would
not produce the changes that needed to occur in schools and classrooms.
They had the answer—job-embedded learning—they just needed a better
strategy for using it.

Fortunately, despite initial skepticism, evidence has continued to sur-
face demonstrating the potential for school-based, job-embedded learning.
And a number of resources have become available to assist educators in
moving from a district-led effort to a school-based enterprise. *Powerful
Professional Development: Building Expertise Within the Four Walls of Your
School* is a valuable guide to be added at the top of your list of such resources.
The authors recognize that when the shift occurs to job-embedded learning,
there is an accompanying shift in the responsibility for planning it.
Effective job-embedded professional development becomes a shared
responsibility among central office, school leaders including teachers, and

external partners. Teacher leaders play a central role in the process; they must serve as advocates, facilitators, coaches, experts, and more. School-based professional development works only when every participant shares the same goals and is willing to be accountable for the results.

There are many aspects to this book that practitioners will appreciate; chief among them is the rare ability of Diane Yendol-Hoppey and Nancy Fichtman Dana to synthesize the work of theorists, trainers, and practitioners alike into organizers that will have meaning for school-based educators. Typically a resource concentrates on theory or practice. Yendol-Hoppey and Dana masterfully balance attention to both with this book that so effectively meets the needs of its audience: school-based leaders who must assume responsibility for professional learning.

I wish I had had a copy of this text when I planned that first professional development experience! Fortunately, many educators now will—and as a result, the experience for their colleagues will be very different and much more positive. As staff development leaders, we have a responsibility to understand the foundations of our field as well as be able to serve the needs of educators with whom we work on a regular basis. *Powerful Professional Development: Building Expertise Within the Four Walls of Your School* helps us achieve both goals. School teams that embrace its message and use its tools will succeed in their efforts to ensure effective job-embedded learning that improves the day-to-day learning and effectiveness of educators and students alike.

Stephanie Hirsh
Executive Director
National Staff Development Council

Preface

In this age of dwindling resources and high-stakes accountability, many schools and districts are feeling pressed for time and squeezed for funds; they are being forced to teach more content in the same amount of time and, most tragically, cut their staff-development budgets in ways that curb opportunities for teacher learning. Yet, according to *The Report of the Task Force on Teacher Leadership* (2001),

> No single principle of school reform is more valid or durable than the maxim that student learning depends first, last, and always on the quality of the teachers. Experts may disagree about how highly to value the size of a class or school, how the system functions, or whether it is adequately funded—but nobody's list of education's priorities fails to place teacher quality at or very near the top. (p. 1)

Hence, even under these current conditions, school districts must focus on the continued learning of their teachers.

Our purpose in this book is to help educators—including teacher leaders, principals, coaches, district staff-development directors, and superintendents, as well as state policy makers—understand how to cultivate powerful job-embedded, professional development opportunities from within the four walls of the school, particularly when time and money are tight. In designing professional development, educators who use this book will learn to accomplish much more with less and garner a higher return rate on staff-development investments they do make.

Our intent is to provide an overview of a number of different strategies that work well for job-embedded professional development and share creative ways to find time and resources to make these different strategies a reality in a school. Rather than providing an in-depth look at one particular strategy or tool, we have collected information about many powerful forms of professional development, so educators can make informed decisions about which strategies are most important for the particular purposes of their work. In crafting this text, we hoped to cultivate a greater understanding of the breadth of powerful job-embedded, professional development strategies educators can have in their toolboxes and a working knowledge of when to pull out which tool for what purpose. This book will help educators match each professional development tool with the particular needs of a school or district, rather than make the case for one approach or another.

Key ideas from both the research literature and practicing educators have shaped the approach to job-embedded professional development that we take in this book.

- First, to create real and lasting change in schools, leadership must come from all members of your school community. We can no longer rely on the principal and leadership teams to make important changes. Thus, teacher leadership must be valued and cultivated within the four walls of your school.
- Second, real change for your students will only come when pressure is paired with clear support. Unfunded mandates cause only frustration and from the onset are doomed for failure. We can and must provide the time and resources to make it possible for teachers to do their important professional learning work.
- Third, improving practice is possible when educators, like you, intentionally and systematically collaborate to enhance student learning.

ABOUT THIS BOOK

This book is organized into three separate parts, each with a distinctive purpose. Part I, "What Is Powerful Job-Embedded Professional Development, and How Can You Make It Happen?" contains three chapters that work together to lay the foundation for an effective job-embedded, professional development program in your school or district. Chapter 1 defines job-embedded professional development and describes a number of important building blocks that are essential to this form of learning. Chapter 2 addresses productive ways teachers and principals can conceptualize their roles and work in schools within a framework of job-embedded learning. Finally, and perhaps most pressing in this age of dwindling resources to support teachers' professional learning, Chapter 3 is devoted to the issues of time and money. This chapter offers practical ideas for garnering the resources necessary for job-embedded learning to unfold in schools.

In Part II of this book we turn to the description of a number of job-embedded professional development strategies. These strategies include book studies, Webinars, podcasts, online libraries, research-in-action days, coteaching, protocols, open-space technology, knowledge cafés, lesson study, teacher inquiry/action research, coaching, and professional learning communities. In Chapters 4 through 10, we define these strategies and include statements from educators across the nation who have used these tools and can attest to their success. We also provide one or more illustrations of what each tool might look like in action as well as additional resources you can turn to for a more in-depth look. Each one of the strategies explicated in the chapters in Part II becomes a tool you can utilize to actualize job-embedded professional learning. As you work your way through these chapters, you will be building a professional toolbox you can use to incorporate job-embedded learning into your work as district staff developer, principal, teacher leader, coach, superintendent, or policy maker.

Finally, Part III of this text helps you utilize your professional development toolbox in effective ways by discussing ways to match professional development strategies with professional development needs (Chapter 11) and ten lessons learned to achieve job-embedded, professional development success (Chapter 12).

This book recognizes that student learning depends on the quality of the teachers who teach them and demonstrates how job-embedded professional learning is the vehicle for enhancing teacher quality. By working your way through this text, you will become better prepared to offer solutions to the dilemmas educators committed to teacher learning face today. The book also illustrates that paying attention to teacher learning by finding the time and tools for job-embedded professional development is the only vehicle that will ultimately enhance student learning in our schools today.

Acknowledgments

Throughout our careers, we have always been passionate about working with other educators to improve learning for all children. We all have had the same goal: providing support to help make good teachers great teachers. The job-embedded, professional development strategies that we write about in this book were taught to us by true trailblazing educators. They are the living evidence that job-embedded professional development can occur in schools when educators are innovative and relentless about demanding, supporting, and honoring teacher and student learning within the school walls.

Hence, this book is possible only because our colleagues were willing to share their professional lives with us by inviting us into their schools and sharing both their celebrations as well as their dilemmas—with honesty. We are grateful to our thoughtful colleagues at the West Virginia Department of Education, Dr. Steve Paine, Dr. Karen Huffman, Donna Peduto, Richard Lawrence, Chuck Heinlein, Nathan Estel, Carla Williamson, Lydia Mccue, and Lisa Yuhl, as well as the trailblazing faculty and leadership at the West Virginia University Professional Development Schools, particularly Superintendent Frank Devono and Director of Staff Development Sandy Duvalt; principals Karen Church, Steve King, Jim Napolio, Pam Gallaher, and Carole Crawford; teachers Jeanne Taylor and Cindy Oliver; and University faculty members Sharon Hayes, Ted Price, Pam Whitehouse, Kaye McCrory, Sarah Steel, Judy Abbott, David Hoppey, Johnna Boylard, and Jason Smith. We also thank P. K. Yonge Developmental Research School, particularly Fran Vandiver, Lynda Hayes, and Rose Pringle; the Alachua County/University of Florida Professional Development Community, particularly Angela Gregory, Kara Dawson, Jim Brandenburg, Kevin Berry, and Lacy Redd; the State College Area School District–Pennsylvania State University Professional Development School Partnership, particularly Jim Nolan, Deirdre Bauer, and Donnan Stoicovy; the Lastinger Center for Learning at University of Florida, particularly Don Pemberton, Alyson Adams, Felicia Moss, and Kathy Dixon; the Broward County Public Schools, particularly Terry Campanella; NSRF faculty, particularly Deb

Bambino and Pete Bermudez; the Duval County Public Schools, particularly Lissa Dunn and Monica McLear; Fairfax County Public Schools, particularly Gail Ritchie; Pinellas County Schools, particularly Carol Thomas and Sylvia Boynton; Collier County Public Schools, particularly Cathy Gould; the Baltimore City Public Schools; and the Montgomery County Public Schools in Maryland. All of these influential educators have been willing to share with us their best ideas about how to help support good teachers in becoming great teachers within the school walls.

In addition, we would like to express our appreciation for the tremendous technical support we received in getting this manuscript written, illustrated, and prepared for publication. Specifically, we thank Shawn Black for his exceptional ability to capture the key themes in the book illustrations; Lisa Barnette for her formatting expertise; Carol Chambers Collins, senior acquisitions editor at Corwin; and her editorial assistants, Brett Ory and Allison Scott, for helping us take this book from conceptualization to print!

Finally, no book can be written without the support of our families. We wrote this book under some of the most unusual work conditions. However, we know that the most important work we do is the work that is with our families. David, Tom, Caran, Billy, Kevin, Greg, and Kirsten, we thank you for your willingness to let us disappear for a while from our lives together to complete this project.

About the Authors

Diane Yendol-Hoppey is currently Professor of Education and Director of the Benedum Collaborative at West Virginia University. Prior to her appointment at West Virginia University, she served as the Coordinator of the University of Florida Elementary Apprenticeship and Professional Development Communities and evaluator of numerous district, state, and national professional development efforts. Before beginning her work in higher education, Diane spent thirteen years as an elementary school teacher in Pennsylvania and Maryland. She holds a PhD in curriculum and instruction from Pennsylvania State University. Diane's current work focuses on developing school-university partnerships committed to cultivating an inquiry stance and a commitment to teacher leadership. Diane received the AERA Division K Early Career Research Award for her ongoing commitment to researching innovative approaches to professional development. She has authored articles in professional journals focusing on creating communities of inquiry, teacher leadership, mentoring, and school-university collaboration, as well as three books with Nancy Dana.

Nancy Fichtman Dana is currently Professor of Education and Director of the Center for School Improvement at the University of Florida, Gainesville. Under her direction, the center promotes and supports practitioner inquiry, or action research, as a core mechanism for school improvement in schools throughout the state. Dana began her career in education as an elementary school teacher in Hannibal Central Schools, New York, and has worked closely with teachers and administrators on action research, building professional learning communities and school-university collaborations in Florida and Pennsylvania since 1990. She has authored numerous articles in professional journals as well as published five books (including three with Diane

Yendol-Hoppey). In 2008, the National Staff Development Council (NSDC) honored Dana and Yendol-Hoppey with the 2008 NSDC Staff Development Book of the Year award for *The Reflective Educator's Guide to Professional Development: Coaching Inquiry-Oriented Learning Communities* (2008), and this writing team continues to enjoy researching and writing together about their passion: powerful professional development for all educators. In addition to her books coauthored with Diane, she is the author of *Leading With Passion and Knowledge: The Principal as Action Researcher* (2009) and the coauthor of *The Power of Teacher Networks* (2009).

PART I

What Is Powerful Job-Embedded Professional Development, and How Can You Make It Happen?

Drawing by Shawn Black.

H ave you ever wondered

- Why is teacher professional development often ineffective?
- What would it take to improve teacher professional development and, subsequently, improve schools?
- What is job-embedded professional development, and what might it look like?

Have you ever heard a teacher say

- I just sat in a three-day workshop. I could have learned what they taught me in three hours!
- How did you do that?
- Can I have a copy of your . . . ?
- I wish they would let us be involved with deciding what we should do next. We are the ones that can make it happen!
- That would be great but there just isn't enough time in the school day!

Have you ever looked at an exemplary teacher and wondered why others didn't know the same strategies?

Have you ever had anyone tell you that the problem with schools is that they forgot to build the back porch?

Our guess is that you are nodding yes, perhaps with the sole exception being the very last question about the *back porch*. In Chapter 2, we will more thoroughly explain this phrase, which we and others have used as a metaphor for the kind of conversational space and professional learning culture we would like to encourage in schools.

The purpose of Part I of this book is to address these and other age-old teacher professional development dilemmas by examining

1. what we know about teacher professional development in general and job-embedded professional development in particular (Chapter 1);

2. how and why we need to create a space in schools for job-embedded professional development (Chapter 2); and

3. how to find the time and resources to make job-embedded professional development a reality in your school (Chapter 3).

After reading Part I of this book, you will be able to

1. articulate the ways job-embedded professional development can lead to effective teaching and learning;

2. understand the roles of a teacher leader and principal within a school building and how these roles support job-embedded professional development; and

3. identify ways to create the necessary resources and time within the school day to make professional learning a part of the daily lives of teachers and administrators.

1

Cultivating Professional Development From Inside the Four Walls of Your School

> *Traditional professional development usually occurs away from the schools site, separate from classroom contexts and challenges in which teachers are expected to apply what they have learned, and often without the necessary support to facilitate transfer of learning.*
>
> —Killion & Harrison, 2006

O ver the past fifty years, educators have learned a great deal about what effective professional development does and does not look like. The research has clearly demonstrated that the popular and, unfortunately, still thriving "sit and get" model of professional development, when used in isolation, is not effective in changing classroom practice (Showers & Joyce, 1995). This traditional model, which relies solely on the sharing of external expertise, is expensive as well as ineffective. Typically, it has taken the form of workshops delivered during inservice days (Cochran-Smith & Lytle, 1999; Fullan, 1991; Lieberman, 1995a, 1995b; Lieberman & Miller, 1990; Sparks & Hirsch, 1997). In these workshops, teachers often learn about new strategies, approaches, and pedagogy from an outside expert, and then they are expected to return to their classrooms and independently implement the new knowledge. Today, teachers and school leaders across the nation have been challenged to replace inefficient and less-effective models of professional development with job-embedded teacher professional development that relies on both honoring and cultivating the inside expertise that resides within a school and district.

SO WHAT IS JOB-EMBEDDED PROFESSIONAL DEVELOPMENT?

The National Staff Development Council (NSDC) has led the way to sweeping changes by demanding that professional development be clearly tied to student learning. It envisions schools as places where "every educator engages in effective professional learning every day so every student achieves" (NSDC, 2009).

This focus on every educator learning every day really highlights the importance of shifting our efforts toward job-embedded professional development. According to NSDC, high-quality professional development is conducted among educators at the school and facilitated by well-prepared school principals and school-based professional development coaches, mentors, or other teacher leaders. Additionally, NSDC's vision of job-embedded professional development is that it "occurs several times per week among established teams of teachers, principals, and other instructional staff members where the teams of educators engage in a continuous cycle of improvement" (NSDC, 2009). The emphasis is on systematic, planned, intentional, and regularly scheduled efforts to embed teacher learning within teachers' daily lives. The importance of preparing school leaders across these roles for this work, as well as creating the structures, time, and resources for the school faculty to engage in it, is imperative to changing teaching practice to enhance student learning.

The changing roles of school leaders and the challenges of time and resources are explored in Chapters 2 and 3. In this chapter, we continue to develop the general concept of job-embedded professional development, which according to NSDC (2009), should

- evaluate student, teacher, and school learning needs through a thorough review of data on teacher and student performance;
- define a clear set of educator learning goals based on the rigorous analysis of the data;
- achieve the educator's learning goals by implementing coherent, sustained, and evidenced-based learning strategies, such as lesson study and the development of formative assessments, that improve instructional effectiveness and student achievement;

- provide job-embedded coaching or other forms of assistance to support the transfer of new knowledge and skills to the classroom;
- regularly assess the effectiveness of the professional development in achieving identified learning goals, improving teaching, and assisting all students in meeting challenging state academic-achievement standards;
- inform ongoing improvements in teaching and student learning; and
- sometimes be supported by external assistance.

By attending to these criteria, you will be more likely to develop a viable and powerful plan that has the potential to positively shift the attitudes and confidence of educators toward accepting learning and creating, implementing, and studying their work within their school day and school walls.

WHAT ARE THE BUILDING BLOCKS FOR JOB-EMBEDDED PROFESSIONAL DEVELOPMENT?

The wisdom of Confucius's famous words about learning—"I hear and I forget. I see and I remember. I do and I understand"—applies as much to our lives as teachers as it does to the education of our students. Although our professional learning often, but not always, begins by hearing about new innovations, the transfer of the innovation to our practice is often complicated due to myriad barriers. Teachers regularly lament, "If I only had the chance to see that idea in action or the time to try it myself, I would both remember and understand."

The act of teaching is highly complex, and this complexity must not be underestimated. As Linda Darling-Hammond (1997b) wisely explains, "effective teaching is not routine, students are not passive, and questions of practice are not simple, predictable, or standardized" (p. 67). To illuminate the great complexity inherent in teaching and, subsequently, in teacher professional development, we explore four different types of building blocks that are necessary for effective job-embedded professional development: knowledge source, knowledge type, orientation, and learning needs. These building blocks draw upon classic discussions of teacher learning that have developed over the last few decades to provide the foundation for understanding the complexity of teacher knowledge.

1 Knowledge Source

One of the most significant frameworks for understanding the role that professional knowledge plays in educational change is put forth by

Cochran-Smith and Lytle (2001, 2009). They offer a radically different view of the role that practitioners play in educational change. The complexity of teaching, as evidenced in a great deal of research, requires that educators interested in making changes in classroom practice must engage in multiple types of knowledge construction. Marilyn Cochran-Smith and Susan Lytle (1999) offered a useful framework to describe three different sources of knowledge teachers need to make lasting and effective changes to their practice.

Knowledge for Practice

The first knowledge source, referred to as *knowledge for practice,* helps educators become informed about new educational-research-based practices that have legitimized their worth. Many times, this source of knowledge comes to teachers in the form of workshops, book studies, speakers, Weblogs, and research articles. Although important to setting the stage for improving practice, the professional development approaches that focus on knowledge for practice provide only limited support for the integration of that new knowledge into the teacher's practice. As Confucius notes, this kind of knowledge can be heard but forgotten and never make its way to classroom practice.

Knowledge in Practice

Given that the knowledge for practice model of professional development offers no mechanism to help teachers understand and address these dilemmas during implementation, educators involved with the professional development of teachers have recognized the importance of a second knowledge source—*knowledge in practice.* Knowledge in practice recognizes the importance of practical knowledge and its role in improving teaching practice. Often, this type of knowledge is generated as teachers begin testing out the knowledge for practice gained from attending an inservice workshop, reading a book, listening to a speaker, or reading a research article. As teachers apply this new knowledge within their classrooms and schools, they construct knowledge *in* practice. Knowledge in practice is strengthened as teachers deliberatively engage in specific teaching episodes, crafting and articulating the tacit or often unarticulated knowledge that emerges from their experiences applying the knowledge for practice. Knowledge in practice is strengthened through collaboration with peers (Cochran-Smith & Lytle, 1999). For example, professional development vehicles including mentoring and peer coaching rely on collaboration and dialogue that can generate reflection, improve implementation, as well as make public the new knowledge being created. Knowledge in practice can result in the teacher being able to both see a research-based practice in action and do a research-based practice, facilitating transfer to practice.

Knowledge of Practice

A third source of knowledge that is gaining attention from professional developers today is *knowledge of practice.* Knowledge of practice stresses that through systematic inquiry "teachers make problematic their own knowledge and practice as well as the knowledge and practice of others" (Cochran-Smith & Lytle, 1999, p. 273). Teachers create this kind of knowledge as they focus on raising questions about and systematically study their own classroom teaching. Cochran-Smith and Lytle suggest, "what goes on inside the classroom is profoundly altered and ultimately transformed when teachers' frameworks for practice foreground the intellectual, social, and cultural contexts of teaching" (p. 276). What this means is that as teachers engage in this third type of knowledge construction, they move beyond the nuts and bolts of classroom practice to examine how these nuts and bolts might reflect larger issues, such as equity that could potentially inhibit student learning. Teachers interested in constructing knowledge of practice receive support as they collaboratively inquire with colleagues using a wide variety of data sources (e.g., assessments, student work, anecdotal records) about how their own teaching practices might inhibit the learning that takes place for all children in their schools and classrooms. In combination, these three sources of knowledge lead to powerful professional learning.

Reflection

As teachers tap into all three sources of knowledge (*for, in,* and *of*), the process of reflection plays a critical role in their learning. Reflection has historically been recognized as a hallmark of educator professional learning; in 1933, educational philosopher John Dewey argued that reflection on our experiences strengthens teacher learning since we learn from those experiences that we ponder, explore, review, and question. Reflection allows teachers to deepen their professional knowledge construction, but the process is more than "just thinking hard about what you do" (Bullough & Gitlin, 1995, p. 35).

Standing on the shoulders of John Dewey, Donald Schön (1983) contributes to our understanding of teacher learning in his discussion of reflection in action and reflection on action. Reflection in action, sometimes referred to as "thinking on your feet," occurs while a teaching episode is happening and is highly connected to the concept of knowledge in practice. This is an intuitive professional activity often based on past professional experience and includes engaging in an ongoing reflective conversation with yourself as you are teaching. Reflection on action occurs after the teaching episode. Reflecting on action enables teachers to explore why they acted as they did and what was happening to the students during the teaching episode. This form of reflection is a part of knowledge of practice. In order for teachers to deepen their professional knowledge in a way that enhances student learning, teachers rely on all three kinds of knowledge sources as they reflect to resolve an uncertainty or perplexity resulting from an innovation. Schön's ideas about reflection help us connect Cochran-Smith and Lytle's ideas with Dewey's concept of reflection offered almost a century ago.

2   Knowledge Type

In addition to sources of knowledge, a second essential building block is knowledge type. Lee Shulman (1987a, 1987b) began a rich conversation focused on the broad types of knowledge teachers must possess and the importance of being able to integrate multiple knowledge domains as they teach. Over time, these domains have grown to include content knowledge, pedagogical knowledge, student knowledge, curriculum knowledge, pedagogical content knowledge, and context knowledge. To engage teachers in effective job-embedded professional development, paying attention to teachers' knowledge development in each one of these areas over time is critical. In this section, we define each type of knowledge.

Content Knowledge

Fairly or unfairly, teachers today are under attack as policy makers claim a lack of content knowledge in our teaching force. Importantly, within educational research, a substantial body of literature exists noting that teachers need a deeper understanding of what they need to teach in order for them to be effective instructional decision makers (Ball & McDiarmid, 1989). Educational researchers Deborah Ball and Bill McDiarmid (1989) specify three aspects of content knowledge essential for teaching. First, the teacher must understand the central facts, concepts, theories, and procedures essential to the lesson content. Second, the teacher must have an explanatory framework that organizes and connects the ideas for both the teacher and the students. Third, the teacher must understand the rules for evidence within the content area.

Pedagogical Knowledge

A second type of professional knowledge focuses on developing general pedagogical expertise that begins by becoming familiar with instructional tools of the trade. Teachers need support as they develop this repertoire of instructional tools, including but not limited to familiarity with standards as well as the ability to plan, deliver, and assess meaningful learning experiences (Wasley, Hampel, & Clark, 1997). According to Feiman-Nemser (2001), "Good teachers know about a range of approaches to curriculum, instruction, and assessment; and they have the judgment, skill, and understanding to decide what to use when" (p. 1018).

Student Knowledge

In addition to understanding content that is being taught and developing a repertoire of instructional strategies, teaching also requires sufficient knowledge about learners in the classroom. Any content or pedagogy can play out very differently depending on the background, experiences, and prior knowledge of each individual learner in the classroom. With knowledge of the students, teachers can effectively differentiate instruction. Getting to know students both individually and collectively is often accomplished through analyzing student work, comparing student success with various curricular materials, interviewing students to better understand their thinking, and reflecting on the differing impact instruction has on different students.

Curriculum Knowledge

Even when teachers have a strong understanding of the students in their classroom, in order to differentiate instruction they must know the curriculum inside and out to make appropriate adjustments based on their students' needs. The process of making those curricular adjustments requires an understanding of the curriculum standards as well as the organization and sequence of the curriculum. Curriculum knowledge also includes being aware of current research on curriculum implications for student learning and negotiating the complexities of high-stakes testing. In today's high-stakes testing environment, any professional development initiative needs to support teachers as they figure out how to teach for conceptual understanding of the subject matter while still attending to the pressures of high-stakes accountability.

Pedagogical Content Knowledge

Although many educators don't use the term *pedagogical content knowledge* (PCK) as they share with others their practical knowledge of teaching, PCK is the most complex type of teacher knowledge. This knowledge is hard to pin down, as it requires the simultaneous integration of many other types of professional knowledge discussed. Pedagogical content knowledge is an elaborate name for the unique knowledge construction that occurs in teachers' minds as they blend their knowledge of the context, content, instructional pedagogy, and their knowledge of their students (Grossman, 1990; Magnusson, Krajcik, & Borko, 1999; Shulman, 1987a, 1987b). This type of teacher knowledge emerges as teachers think about how to connect a specific subject matter to students with diverse backgrounds and academic needs within a school characterized by limited resources and significant accountability pressures, while at the same time monitoring for misconceptions that students may develop.

Context Knowledge

Finally, the importance of understanding the organization in which one teaches should not be underestimated. Figuring out school politics on top of trying to meet the needs of every student each day is essential to teaching effectively within a school system. Context knowledge includes but is not limited to understanding district and curriculum policy, school scheduling and grouping practices, the principal's leadership style, the school's mission and vision, each educator's roles and responsibilities in the building, and the community that surrounds the school. Additionally, teachers need to gain access to the professional language and dialogue of the school, knowledge of resources available and who controls those resources, and the language of education reform.

In many school systems, accountability pressures have created staff-development shifts that marginalize the complexity and types of professional knowledge and focus on increased "training" to encourage fidelity to the implementation of new commercial texts that promise to boost student performance. Yet, textbooks rarely offer professional development that integrates a teacher's understanding of content, pedagogical, student, curriculum, pedagogical content, and context knowledge. Most textbooks are scripted, and teachers are often encouraged to adhere to a curriculum that does not accommodate all of their students' learning needs. Only a teacher who knows how to monitor student learning during his or her instruction will be positioned to integrate these multiple types of teacher knowledge. Job-embedded professional development takes into account all six types of knowledge as teachers learn in practice with one another's support.

3   Orientation

It's important to note that job-embedded professional development must recognize, value, and integrate two different and somewhat opposite orientations to developing our professional knowledge base. The first approach consists of teachers becoming skilled in implementing research-based practices generated by other educators in the field and systematically studied (Marzano, Pickering, & Pollock, 2001), referred to as *outside* knowledge. The second approach insists on teachers drawing on their own craft knowledge to suggest new innovations for systematic study with the promise of contributing to the research base (Cochran-Smith & Lytle, 2009; Dana & Yendol-Hoppey, 2008). This is referred to as *inside* knowledge. Job-embedded professional development that embraces these two orientations recognizes the complexity of teaching and provides the opportunity for teachers to not only enhance student learning but also participate in professional knowledge construction.

4 Learning Needs

The fourth building block recognizes the importance of attending to teacher learning needs as we provide opportunities for job-embedded learning. Research indicates that change takes time and support (Banilower & Shimkus, 2004; Fullan, 2001a, 2001b). Instructional change that is real, lasting, and meaningful requires shifts in school culture. Professional development during this era must encourage a set of qualitative shifts in the way schools work. The development of teacher professional knowledge and instructional changes that will help all children learn takes time. Laura Desimone (2009) and Hilda Borko (2004) argue that attending to teacher learning needs requires differentiating between passive learning, which is typically listening to a lecture, and active learning, which includes the process of observing expert teachers or being observed, engaging in interactive feedback and discussion, reviewing student work, and leading discussion.

Similarly, drawing specifically on the work of Bruce Joyce and Beverly Showers (1995), the most powerful combination of teacher activities that will ultimately create shifts in practice is a combination of five professional learning needs that, when addressed, lead to changes in teaching practice. These needs include

1. developing understanding of research-based practices, possible innovations, and the underlying theory and evidence that elevates them to being worthwhile of educator attention;

2. providing opportunities for demonstration or modeling of the practice;

3. affording teachers the time to practice the innovation;

4. creating opportunities for feedback and coaching; and

5. creating collaborative conditions that encourage reflection on the outcomes of the work.

By attending to each of these five professional learning needs, we create a *theory of change*, which identifies the steps, the connections between learning activities, and the outcomes that occur at each stage. Professional development is stronger when a theory of change guides the planning process, and defining a theory of change allows educators the power to improve their instruction and, ultimately, improve learning for all students.

In sum, there exist four different types of building blocks that are necessary for effective job-embedded professional development: knowledge source, knowledge type, orientation, and learning needs. Table 1.1 summarizes these different types of building blocks and illustrates what is

Table 1.1 Building Blocks for Powerful Professional Learning

Building-Block Type	Building Blocks						Theorists
Learning Needs	Understanding of research-based practice	View model	Practice time	Feedback and coaching	Collaborative conversation and reflection		Borko (2004); Desimone (2009); Joyce and Showers (1983)
Orientation	Outside orientation			Inside orientation			Marzano, Pickering, and Pollock (2001); Cochran-Smith and Lytle (1999, 2001, 2009)
Type of Knowledge	Pedagogical knowledge	Curriculum knowledge	Student knowledge	Content knowledge	Context knowledge	Pedagogical content knowledge	Ball and McDiarmid (1989); Grossman (1990); Magnusson, Krajcik, and Borko (1999); Shulman (1987a, 1987b)
Source of Knowledge	Knowledge for practice		Knowledge in practice		Knowledge of practice		Cochran-Smith and Lytle (1999, 2001, 2009); Dewey (1933); Schön (1983)

needed when building a foundation and framework for meaningful and powerful job-embedded professional development. Enacting job-embedded professional development means accounting for all of the building blocks at some point as a school's or district's professional development plan unfolds over the course of the school year. Staff developers, whether they are principals, teacher leaders, or district specialists, utilize all of the building blocks by matching professional development tools to the learning needs of teachers in their schools and districts.

With so many essential building blocks, creating powerful professional development is a tremendously complex endeavor. We'll explore a variety of learning tools in Part II of this book. But first, we explore the story of Mrs. Oublier—a mathematics teacher who was studied and described in a seminal case study completed by David Cohen (1990) two decades ago—to illustrate what can happen when the complexity of teacher professional development is underestimated. In sharing this story, we exemplify the important role that each professional learning building block plays in developing a new professional practice.

AN EXAMPLE: WHAT DID MRS. OUBLIER TEACH US ABOUT BUILDING PROFESSIONAL KNOWLEDGE THAT FACILITATES CHANGE?

In the mid-1980s, California State officials launched an ambitious effort to enhance mathematics teaching and learning. The aim was to shift the curriculum from promoting mechanical memorization to promoting mathematical understanding, and this shift would require attention to each of the professional learning building blocks. Mrs. Oublier was one of those teachers participating in the mathematics reform. David Cohen (1990) explains,

> Mrs. Oublier reported that when she began work four years ago, her mathematics teaching was thoroughly traditional. She followed the text. Her second graders spent most of their time on worksheets. Learning math meant memorizing facts and procedures. Then Mrs. O found a new way to teach math. She took a workshop in which she learned to focus lessons on students' understanding of mathematical ideas. She found ways to relate mathematical concepts to students' knowledge and experience. And she explored methods to engage students in actively understanding mathematics. In her third year of such work, Mrs. O was delighted with her students' performance, and with her own accomplishments. (p. 311)

As indicated, Mrs. Oublier engaged in a workshop and then spent the next few years independently working out how to implement this new instructional orientation. She believed that she had revolutionized her teaching.

As her mathematics teaching story unfolds, Mrs. Oublier appears less successful in her ability to move the ideas from the workshop she attended to her classroom in a way that truly reforms her mathematics instruction. This well-intended, motivated, and enthusiastic teacher "believes that she has revolutionized her mathematics teaching. But observations of her classroom reveals that the innovations in her teaching have been filtered through a very traditional approach to instruction" (p. 311).

So, what went awry in Mrs. Oublier's professional development? The shaded building blocks in Table 1.2 indicate the only areas of professional development that were systematically attended to in planning Mrs. Oublier's professional development. One lesson we learn from Mrs. Oublier is that teachers have a formidable task in not only learning new approaches but "unlearning" their existing teaching as well. Mrs. Oublier had to learn a new approach to teaching mathematics based on a very different theoretical and conceptual foundation, but she did not have access to the building blocks necessary to create that instructional change. For example, Mrs. Oublier did not receive coaching feedback or have the opportunity for collaborative learning. She was not pressed to articulate the knowledge *in* and *of* practice she was constructing through systematic study. Mrs. Oublier also did not possess an inside orientation toward professional learning as she relied on external knowledge which she believed she was implementing with fidelity.

Drawing on external knowledge introduced by the mathematics reform, she began developing new curriculum, content, and pedagogical knowledge while simultaneously letting go of what she believed were tried-and-true approaches to mathematics instruction. Despite her commitment to learning, her practice could only change on the surface. Until she was able to shed her existing teaching methods as well as understand and embrace each of the knowledge types in a way that cultivated pedagogical content knowledge, she would be unable to implement the mathematics reform effectively. What we learn from Mrs. Oublier is that although knowledge *for* practice remains essential to shifting belief systems and making authentic change, knowledge *for* practice is not enough to realize deep and real change in classroom instruction and student learning.

Today, we don't have to relearn the lessons that Mrs. Oublier has taught us. We have a deeper understanding of the complexity associated with helping teachers shift established teaching practices. Drawing on lessons learned in this book, Mrs. Oublier would receive more support today than she did many years ago. Specifically, we would create time and structured opportunities for her to become intimately aware of the

Table 1.2   What Happened to Mrs. Oublier? Missing Building Blocks

Building-Block Type	*Building Blocks*						*Theorists*
Learning Needs	Understanding of research-based practice		View model	Practice time	Feedback and coaching	Collaborative conversation and reflection	Borko (2004); Desimone (2009); Joyce and Showers (1983)
Orientation	Outside orientation			Inside orientation			Marzano, Pickering, and Pollock (2001); Cochran-Smith and Lytle (1999, 2001, 2009)
Type of Knowledge	Pedagogical knowledge	Curriculum knowledge	Student knowledge	Content knowledge	Context knowledge	Pedagogical content knowledge	Ball and McDiarmid (1989); Grossman (1990); Magnusson, Krajcik, and Borko (1999); Shulman (1987a, 1987b)
Source of Knowledge	Knowledge for practice		Knowledge in practice		Knowledge of practice		Cochran-Smith and Lytle (1999, 2001, 2009); Dewey (1933); Schön (1983)

theoretical and conceptual underpinnings of the new technique. She might engage in book studies, watch a podcast, and attend a workshop. She would also be provided with multiple opportunities to watch other teachers model the new orientation to mathematics as well as debrief the observation together, studying the link that exists between new theoretical and conceptual understandings and the new teaching practice. These kinds of activities would be done with a focus on making sure Mrs. Oublier understood the change deeply and had created a belief system aligned with the innovation. These kinds of activities meet the challenges described in the first two types of professional learning needs (understanding of research-based practices and opportunities to demonstrate or model) as well as create knowledge for practice.

Once Mrs. Oublier developed knowledge for practice, we would begin providing her support structures, such as content-focused coaching, to help her create knowledge in practice. To fulfill the professional learning need for practice, feedback, and coaching, Mrs. Oublier would plan the lesson with a content-focused coach, implement the mathematics instruction with the coach observing, discuss her dilemmas, and receive feedback on the instructional episode.

Today, Mrs. Oublier could also be supported by a professional learning community (PLC) of teachers interested in collectively reforming their approach to teaching mathematics. Meeting together on a regular basis and within the school day, the PLC would help shape Mrs. Oublier's knowledge of practice. Mrs. Oublier would have access to opportunities to collaboratively reflect on the practice with colleagues in light of broader educational and societal issues. Only by looking at an innovation through multiple lenses, creating a critical mass of teachers using the innovation, and raising questions about the innovation's usefulness for improving learning for all children will large-scale improvements occur in student learning. Given our new knowledge of professional learning today, Mrs. Oublier would have been much more likely to be successful in shifting her practice.

CONCLUDING THOUGHTS

The lessons that those interested in developing powerful professional development can learn from this chapter include the following:

1. Utilizing and sharing widely the National Staff Development Council's (2009) "bold new approach to job-embedded professional development" to create support for job-embedded professional development within your school

2. Recognizing the complexity of professional learning described by Linda Darling-Hammond (1987)

3. Tapping the three sources of knowledge (for, in and of practice) discussed by Marilyn Cochran-Smith and Susan Lytle (1999, 2009)

4. Understanding the importance and meaning of reflection in action and reflection on action and how it relates to all three knowledge sources as discussed by Donald Schön (1983)

5. Addressing all six types of knowledge (content, pedagogical, student, curriculum, pedagogical content, and context) discussed by Lee Shulman (1987a, 1987b) and others

6. Continually balancing and encouraging the interaction of both an *outside* and *inside* orientation to professional development by encouraging two kinds of teacher involvement in school improvement:
   - Teachers becoming skilled in implementing research-based practices generated by other educators (*outside* to *inside*)
   - Teachers drawing on their craft knowledge to suggest new innovations that they systematically study (*inside* to *outside*)

7. Planning for all five professional learning needs (understanding research-based practices, opportunities to demonstrate or model, practice time, feedback and coaching, and collaborative conditions) discussed by Beverly Showers and Bruce Joyce (1995)

8. Not underestimating the importance of teachers understanding and embracing the theoretical and conceptual underpinnings of an instructional practice as illustrated by Mrs. Oublier (as discussed in Cohen, 1990)

In sum, this chapter helps us understand both the importance and the complexity involved in cultivating professional development from inside the four walls of your school. Advocates for this form of job-embedded professional development, Joellen Killion and Cindy Harrison (2006), remind us of how important teacher learning is to student learning: "District and school administrators know students are not likely to perform at higher levels until teachers begin performing at higher levels" (p. 8). We end this chapter with an exercise to help you begin paying attention to the content presented by thinking about your own professional development experiences as well as future job-embedded professional development that will set you and your school up for successful teacher learning.

Exercise 1.1   The Building Blocks for Job-Embedded Professional Learning

Step 1: Describe the most powerful professional development experience that you have engaged in during your career:

_____

_____

_____

_____

_____

_____

_____

_____

_____

Step 2: Review Table 1.1 and identify which building blocks were incorporated into your most powerful professional development experience. Use the checklist below as you consider your powerful professional development experience in light of the building blocks of job-embedded learning:

Sources of Knowledge (Marilyn Cochran-Smith & Susan Lytle, 1999)

☐ Knowledge for practice
☐ Knowledge in practice
☐ Knowledge of practice

Reflection (Donald Schön, 1983)

☐ Reflection in action
☐ Reflection on action

Types of Knowledge (Lee Shulman, 1987a, 1987b)

☐ Content knowledge
☐ Pedagogical knowledge
☐ Student knowledge
☐ Curriculum knowledge
☐ Pedagogical content knowledge
☐ Context knowledge

Outside/Inside Orientations (Robert Marzano, Debra Pickering, & Jane Pollock, 2001)

☐ Outside
☐ Inside

Learning Needs (Bruce Joyce & Beverly Showers, 1983)

☐ Understanding research-based practice
☐ Opportunities to demonstrate or model
☐ Practice time
☐ Feedback and coaching time
☐ Collaborative conditions

Step 3: Analyze the checkmarks in Step 2. In what ways might your most powerful professional learning experience have been even better had some of the nonchecked building blocks of job-embedded professional learning been incorporated into your experience?

Step 4: Consider your school's or district's current professional development practices. In what ways are they similar to and different from the most powerful professional development experience you described in Step 1? What are your recommendations for improving your school's or district's professional development practices based on the concepts presented in this chapter?

ADDITIONAL RESOURCES

Web Sites

National Staff Development Council. http://www.nsdc.org.

Publications

Cochran-Smith, M., & Lytle, S. L. (1993). *Inside/outside: Teacher research and knowledge.* New York: Teachers College Press.

Cochran-Smith, M., & Lytle, S. L. (1999). Relationships of knowledge and practice: Teacher learning in communities. *Review of Research in Education, 24,* 249–305.

Cochran-Smith, M., & Lytle, S. L. (2001). Beyond certainty: Taking an inquiry stance on practice. In A. Lieberman & L. Miller (Eds.), *Teachers caught in the action: Professional development that matters* (pp. 45–58). New York: Teachers College Press.

Cohen, D. K. (1990). A revolution in one classroom: The case of Mrs. Oublier. *Educational Evaluation and Policy, 12*, 311–325.

Dana, N. F., & Yendol-Hoppey, D. (2008). *The reflective educator's guide to professional development: Coaching inquiry-oriented learning communities.* Thousand Oaks, CA: Corwin.

Joyce, B. R., & Showers, B. (1983). *Power in staff development through research on training.* Alexandria, VA: Association of Supervision and Curriculum Development.

Marzano, R., Pickering, D., & Pollock, J. (2001). *Classroom instruction that works: Research-based strategies for increasing student achievement.* Alexandria, VA: McCrel.

Schön, D. (1983). *The reflective practitioner: How professionals think in action.* London: Temple Smith.

Shulman, L. S. (1987, Spring). Knowledge and teaching: Foundations of the new reform. *Harvard Educational Review*, 1–22.

Shulman, L. S. (1987). The wisdom of practice: Managing complexity in medicine and teaching. In D. C. Berliner & B. V. Rosenshire (Eds.), *Talks to teachers: A festschrift for N. L. Gage* (pp. 369–384). New York: Random House.

2

Creating Space and Reconceptualizing Roles for Job-Embedded PD

Building the Back Porch

American schools and the people who work in them are being asked to do something new—to engage in systematic, continuous improvement in the quality of educational experience of students and to subject themselves to the discipline of measuring their success by the metric of students' academic performance. Most people who currently work in public schools weren't hired to do this work, nor have they been adequately prepared to do it either by their professional education or by their prior experience in schools.

—Elmore, 2002

We have explored the key features of professional development (PD) supported by the National Staff Development Council as well as the key building blocks needed to create a theory of instructional change. In this chapter, we will explore two key ideas: (1) the need to utilize the four different types of building blocks discussed in Chapter 1 to create a space, which we refer to metaphorically as the "back porch," for professionals to meet and converse about teaching and learning, and (2) the importance of reconfiguring the roles of educators as they sit and converse on the back porch. Together, these two undertakings—the creation of a space and the rethinking of roles—form the necessary foundation for the effective facilitation of job-embedded professional development.

As noted in the opening quote to this chapter, you likely weren't hired to engage in the important work of job-embedded professional learning. Therefore, thinking about the notions of space and roles will be essential to help you and your colleagues engage in school reform even though you may not have been adequately prepared to do so by your education or your prior experience in schools. So, let's build the back porch together!

WHAT EXACTLY IS A SCHOOL'S BACK PORCH?

Our professional friends in West Virginia shared the back-porch metaphor with us. As the story goes, well-known spokesperson for Effective Schools, Larry Lezotte, in a conversation with the state superintendent Steven Paine and others boldly proclaimed,

> In the social architecture of the American Public Schools, we have failed to adequately build the "back porch." When we moved from the one room school house of the past to the more complex arrangement of today's schools, we built no collegial arrangement where teachers could collectively reflect on the day's activities and results and subsequently discuss what would be improved tomorrow.

Although this may sound like an unusual metaphor for thinking about schools, the metaphor does help us highlight the power of conversation in helping educators create solutions to pressing problems.

To illustrate the power of conversation on the back porch, Diane fondly recalls her childhood experiences:

> As a child, I can remember visiting my Grandma's house and waking up to find my mom and my Grandma sitting on the porch talking about all sorts of family-related stuff. It seemed like they could solve any problem together.
>
> When I was lying in bed at night with the window open, I would hear my father and his friends in the neighborhood talking about problems in the community and at his local shop. The back porch allowed the men to slow down and have a good visit.

On Sunday afternoon, neighborhood families strolling by would ring the bell, and mom and dad would invite them in for lemonade on the back porch. The kids would play in the yard while the adults would talk about the dilemmas they were experiencing in raising the kids and paying the bills.

I think my very favorite back-porch memory was the time when my grandmother sat with my friends and me on the back porch. I was a teenager, and my friends and I were hashing out some silly teenage conflict. My grandmother sat quietly knitting on the swing listening to us. After some time, she began asking us some questions about what had happened. You know, she never had to tell us what she thought about our conversation because by the time she finished asking us questions, we had figured out how silly our conversation was in the first place, and we turned our conversation to something much more productive. She and so many others, at unexpected times, brought so much wisdom to our lives on that back porch.

Every member of our family and many of our neighbors have spent some time on our back porch expressing themselves with heartache and tears, joy and laughter, as well as struggles and anxiety. Advice and support was offered there. These were conversations about life, and these conversations improved the quality of our lives, the way we worked, lived, and played with others. Within these conversations, we heard different advice, tools, and ways of thinking, depending on the dilemma or topic.

Diane's childhood recollections emphasize the importance of creating time for people to sit and visit. The "back porch" is many things. It is the place where, surrounded by family and friends, you can talk about your hopes, dreams, worries, and fears within a safe and trusting environment. It is the place where life's dilemmas are collaboratively explored and solved. It is the place that represents a time when the world wasn't so busy and people could sit and make time for lengthy, get-beneath-the-surface conversations about what was happening in the world, country, state, or even just down the street.

Unfortunately, the pace of life has sped up to the point that it is difficult to replicate back-porch activity, either in life or in schools. However, to create the conditions for powerful professional learning to happen in schools, we can't afford *not* to find the time and resources to create the "back porch" that Larry Lezotte identified as missing. Consider the following eight characteristics of these unhurried learning conversations from Diane's childhood reflections. Back-porch conversations

1. require time for thoughtful consideration of a situation or issue;

2. can facilitate change;

3. allow us to make problems transparent within a context of trust and safety;

4. are filled with questions and silences in which we ponder multiple perspectives that allow deeper and more sophisticated problem solving and the possibilities for resolution;

5. support the generation of new knowledge through collaborative dialogue and problem solving;

6. are better when there is wisdom in the words;

7. serve a variety of purposes and allow a variety of approaches; and

8. bring together different individuals with unique and important contributions to make to the conversation.

We feel the back-porch metaphor holds true when we apply these lessons to job-embedded professional development. This conversational space gives teachers and administrators a place to

- thoughtfully consider situations and issues that arise from practice;
- facilitate change to best meet the ever-evolving academic, social, and emotional needs of students;
- articulate problems of practice in a safe and trusting environment;
- provide opportunities for educators to both share and listen and in so doing consider multiple resolutions and perspective related to educational problems;
- construct new knowledge about teaching and learning;
- share wisdom acquired from years of classroom experience with one another;
- serve a number of different purposes for teacher professional learning and select from a number of different professional learning strategies to match the purpose at hand; and
- bring a teacher or administrator's own unique and important individual contributions to collective conversations about teaching and learning in schools.

Simply put, job-embedded professional development is all about building that missing back porch in schools.

In the next chapter, we provide ideas for finding the money and time to build your porch. In Part II of this text, we share professional development tools for professional learning that can occur there. First, however, we close this chapter with a brief look at the people who will congregate on the school's back porch—teachers and administrators—and the ways their roles must change for powerful professional learning to come to life in your school.

WHO IS ON THE BACK PORCH? ROLES AND RESPONSIBILITIES

As the school back porch is "constructed," both teachers and principals face important shifts in their work roles. For example, the teacher must assume new roles, such as teacher as researcher, teacher as collaborator, teacher as decision maker, and teacher as coach. Encompassing all of these roles is the overarching role of teacher leader. Additionally, principals must embrace and model the disposition of head learner and creative-resource manager. These are central behaviors to assuring that quality job-embedded professional development occurs within a school. In the next sections of this chapter, we further explore the roles of teacher as leader as well as principal as head learner and creative-resource manager.

WHAT IS A TEACHER LEADER?

Three waves of scholarship and practice have shaped the shoreline of teacher leadership during the last few decades (Silva, Gimbert, & Nolan, 2000). In the first wave, teacher leadership relied on teachers assuming formal positions, such as department chair, site-committee member, or union representative, and these positions largely focused on increasing the efficiency of school management. Activities included scheduling, assigning classes, coordinating special events, and serving as a communication link between administrators and teachers. In this wave, conceptions of teacher leaders focused on keeping things running smoothly.

The second wave of teacher leadership recognized the importance of teachers as instructional leaders, and schools created positions that capitalized on teachers' instructional knowledge. Teachers now assumed formally identified leadership positions, such as staff developer or curriculum specialist. Typically, these instructional-leadership functions were add-ons or replacements to regular classroom teaching responsibilities; curricular or instructional leadership remained outside teachers' central role.

Today, we embrace a third wave of teacher leadership where teachers are leaders in both creating and sustaining a collaborative culture of learning in schools focused on improving instructional practice (Silva et al., 2000). This wave views all teachers as potential leaders who can share the responsibility of continual school improvement targeted at student learning. This form of teacher leadership embraces the notion of leadership from the classroom.

In discussing these waves, Jennifer York-Barr and Karen Duke (2004) note,

> These three waves of teacher leadership reflect an evolution in thinking about how teachers participate in school leadership and

learning. This evolution has not happened in a vacuum. Increasing educational accountability, progressive conceptions of leadership as collective, and the movement to transform schools into professional learning communities are significant contextual influences. (p. 260)

Given the shifting waves of teacher leadership across the decades, the term continues to suffer from definitional problems. Teacher leadership as a part of rather than apart from the role of classroom teacher suggests that the *daily work* of a teacher is not limited to isolated student instruction within the classroom. Rather, teacher leadership is *grounded in work with students,* but this work inside the classroom *spills outside its walls* as teacher leaders share with other educators what they have learned with and from their students. A teacher leader is one who demonstrates commitment to the learning of all students by achieving a high standard of professional excellence in the classroom and by working within the school to create a community of learners who grow professionally and who work collectively to improve the overall effectiveness of the school.

Although we do not advocate that a teacher leader must have a particular degree or credential to lead, we concur with Killion and Harrison (2006) that teacher leaders must be better prepared to serve as exemplary practitioners; mentors of novice and new teachers; reading, math, or academic coaches; professional learning community facilitators; action research coaches; professional development coordinators; team leaders or department chairs; and National Board for Professional Teaching Standards Certified Mentors. The work that today's teacher leaders must do is difficult and complex but equally rewarding as they see teachers take charge of their own professional development.

Teachers are leaders when they collaborate to affect student learning, contribute to school improvement, inspire excellence in practice, and encourage stakeholders to participate in educational improvement (Childs-Bowen, Moller, & Scrivner, 2000). This important work includes assuming roles such as the following:

- Teacher as exemplary practitioner
- Teacher as learner and inquirer
- Teacher as teacher educator
- Teacher as decision maker
- Teacher as collaborator
- Teacher as advocate

Patricia Wasley (1991) wrote almost two decades ago that teacher leadership is the ability to engage colleagues in experimentation and examination of more powerful instructional practices in the service of more engaged student learning. This work requires a new kind of teacher leader. Linda Lambert (1998) explains that teacher leaders "choose integrity over urgency, autonomy and discretion over control, complexity over simplicity, and an emphasis on reciprocal purposeful learning in communities for adults and children" (p. 191). These are the teacher-leadership qualities that can lead to the authentic school improvement described by Jennifer York-Barr and her colleagues (2008) when they remind us that teacher leadership now explicitly places developing learning capacity as its core function by focusing on both learning for the grown-ups *and* students in schools.

This new wave of teacher leadership will require us to utilize the building blocks of powerful job-embedded professional development discussed in Chapter 1 to build back porches equipped for teacher leaders to engage in

> experimentation and examination of more powerful learning activities with and for students, in the service of enhanced student productions and performances of knowledge and understanding. Based on this leadership with and of students, teacher leaders invite other teachers to similar engagements with students in the learning process. (Sergiovanni & Starratt, 2002, p. 149)

Now that we have defined the importance and role of a teacher leader, you can see why teacher leadership is key to engaging in and leading job-embedded, professional development efforts. If you are a teacher leader, you will be primarily responsible for the quality of professional conversation, activity, and reflection that occurs on the back porch that your school builds. These activities are the backbone of any school change efforts that realize enhanced student learning. If teachers' roles shift to being responsible for leading the adult learning that occurs on the back porch of the school, then what happens to the role definition for the person who has traditionally been looked upon as the school leader?

WHAT IS THE ROLE OF THE PRINCIPAL?

According to Roland Barth (1990), principals need the same type of professional development opportunities as teachers, and the best thing they can do for their school is to become the "head learner":

> Sustaining the development of school leaders is crucial to the quality of life and to the best interests of all who inhabit the schoolhouse—and to their development as a community of learners. Principals, no less than teachers, need replenishment and

invigoration and an expanded repertoire of ideas and practices with which to respond to staggering demands. . . . The principal need no longer be the "headmaster" or "instructional leader" pretending to know all. The more crucial role of the principal is as head learner, engaging in the most important enterprise of the schoolhouse—experiencing, displaying, modeling, and celebrating what it is hoped and expected that teachers and pupils will do. (pp. 46, 73)

Head Learner

As head learner, the principal develops the school as a learning organization, so everyone in the organization is developing. That includes listening and learning from and with the school faculty as well as other administrators. As head learner, the principal shares leadership with the professional staff in a way that makes it "our" organization. However, just because we have noted the importance of this role in educational change doesn't mean that we have actualized the role for principals in significant ways within all schools.

In the last decade, scholars have studied principal practices that support the cultivation of the kind of learning illustrated in the back-porch metaphor. Linda Lambert (2000) coined the concept of *constructivist leadership,* and Jim Spillane (2008) articulates the idea of *distributive leadership.* Lambert approaches leadership as a reciprocal process: Through collaboration and relationship building, the school community is able to construct common purpose and processes for reaching shared goals. Similarly, Jim Spillane defines distributive leadership as cultivating both formal and informal leaders through the interaction between all stakeholders and their situations. As you can see, these approaches overlap in that they both seek to involve all stakeholders in the work of improving student learning. Simply put, the lesson here is that the more help a principal gets, the better and the more buy in the principal receives, the more successful the change effort!

To illustrate constructivist and distributive leadership in action, we turn to the work of Steven King, a principal at Mountainview Elementary in Morgantown, West Virginia. The following excerpt from expanded field notes Diane took as a part of a study on principal leadership illustrates how this elementary school approached the dilemma of improving student engagement:

Yesterday, the Mountainview elementary team met to begin studying the topic of student engagement and created a plan to improve student engagement in Tier 1 for RtI (Response to Intervention). What an exciting place to be! What I witnessed was what I would define as a true learning community that demonstrated the concept of simultaneous renewal, created shared knowledge, and reflected mutual respect for all participants. Most of all, the talk was about ways to improve teaching and learning for kids!

Gathered in the conference room were the principal, coaches, the guidance counselor, teachers, a psychology doctoral student interested in child behavior, and myself (a university faculty member who studies teacher professional development and student engagement).

The group meeting began by reviewing a set of essential questions that the school educators had previously identified to guide their work during the 2009 to 2010 academic year. This time, the question or dilemma that was brought first for discussion was from Steve, the principal. He asked, "How should we address Tier 1 behavior, and how will we know when we have it right?" His introduction took about three minutes.

The group responded by presenting three different curriculum tools that might help with the dilemma. Each presenter introduced and described the curriculum or innovation they brought. After presenting, others asked clarifying and probing questions to more fully understand the strengths and weaknesses of the programs.

Many times the participants raised questions about what the research says about the curriculum as well as what kind of curriculum works for what kind of child. Sometimes, this question was asked and answered by a school faculty member; other times, the principal jumped in; and sometimes this question was asked or answered by a university partner. This stage took about ten minutes for each curriculum presentation and questions, resulting in a total of thirty minutes.

After a period of questioning, the group engaged in discussion about the programs and shared their opinions. As the group discussed, the principal listened and took notes while sitting quietly. Periodically, he asked a question or provided a clarifying answer. This phase took about ten minutes.

Once the group had engaged in discussion, the principal reviewed the notes he had taken with the group, summarizing the key concepts and assumptions that had been raised in the discussion, and he asked for their opinions. This took approximately ten minutes.

Finally, the principal asked for the group to come to consensus about their decision related to curriculum. By the conclusion of this discussion, the group members had decided on how they would integrate multiple curricula to meet the range of needs that they had identified. This stage also took about ten more minutes.

As indicated, in one hour, this team had engaged in substantive shared curriculum decision making and knowledge construction related to improving response to intervention Tier 1 behavior concerns. During this time, the principal facilitated a group of educators with diverse roles and expertise as they explored a focus question, presented curriculum, asked clarifying and probing questions, engaged in open discussion, summarized key concepts and assumptions, and built consensus. The group worked collaboratively and the principal positioned himself as head learner, through facilitation as well as listening. Like Steve, if you are a principal, you will be primarily responsible for modeling a learning stance as well as encouraging quality professional conversation, activity, and reflection on the back porch that your school builds. This is the leadership quality that will set the stage for school change efforts and student learning.

Resource Manager

In addition to the responsibility of becoming head learner, the principal is probably the best positioned within the school to garner and dedicate resources to support successful job-embedded professional development and lead teachers in the creative use of time and money within the school to make job-embedded professional development a reality. How one thinks about and uses time and money is a primary factor that either sets teachers up for successful job-embedded professional development experiences or sets them up for failure or frustration. Because of the importance of time and money in relationship to teacher professional development, we dedicate the next chapter solely to exploring this issue.

CONCLUDING THOUGHTS

In this chapter, we have explored how those interested in job-embedded professional development can create space and reconceptualize roles that will generate powerful teacher learning. The back-porch metaphor represents the importance of finding ways for teachers to dialogue about teaching and learning as they create knowledge for, in, and of practice. By taking time to set the stage for this type of work, we are positioned to enhance the learning of all who spend time within the school walls. This chapter ends with three exercises to help you begin the process of building your own back porch and reconceptualizing your own roles as teacher and administrator in your school, so powerful back-porch conversations can happen!

Exercise 2.1   Assessing Your Current Teacher-Leadership Context

Use the Likert scale to rate the role teacher leaders play in your school.

Teacher leaders . . .	1 Not involved	2	3 Somewhat involved	4	5 Highly involved
Redesign instruction based on student assessment.					
Share ideas with colleagues.					
Are a mentor to new teachers.					
Help make personnel decisions.					
Create partnerships with community, families, and universities.					
Facilitate professional learning communities.					
Select professional development.					
Present workshops to colleagues.					
Influence school budgeting.					
Collaborate with peers.					
Lead school committees.					
Collaboratively reflect on teaching practice.					
Initiate school activities.					
Influence school policy.					

Based on these ratings, what recommendations would you have to strengthen teacher leadership at your school?

_____

_____

_____

Exercise 2.2   Administrator Role: A Reflection

Design a timeline of your growth and development as a principal and a leader, beginning with your first teaching position and noting years and dates of critical incidents that impacted your decision to become an administrator and the development of your leadership skills along the way. Once the timeline is completed, extend the timeline ten years into the future with your goal of becoming known as the head learner and creative resource manager of your school. What types of experiences will need to appear on your timeline from the present day throughout the next decade of your career for this goal to be achieved?

Exercise 2.3   Building Your Own Back Porch

Step 1: Consider the eight actions that teachers and administrators can engage in during a back-porch conversation. On a scale from 1 to 10, with 10 representing an activity that occurs extremely frequently, 5 indicating the activity that occurs occasionally, and 1 indicating that the activity never occurs, rate each activity below.

_____ Thoughtfully consider situations and issues that arise from practice

_____ Facilitate change to best meet the ever-evolving academic, social, and emotional needs of students

_____ Articulate problems of practice in a safe and trusting environment

_____ Provide opportunities for educators to both share and listen, and in so doing, consider multiple resolutions and perspective related to educational problems

_____ Construct new knowledge about teaching and learning

_____ Share wisdom acquired from years of classroom experience with one another

_____ Serve a number of different purposes for teacher professional learning and select from a number of different professional learning strategies to match the purpose at hand

_____ Bring a teacher or administrator's own unique and important individual contributions to collective conversations about teaching and learning in schools

Reflect on your ratings of each of these activities. Which activities are already happening? Which activities are present, but need to be enhanced? Which activities need to be introduced into the culture of your school?

Step 2: Gather together a group of your colleagues who are also interested in job-embedded professional learning to discuss the following scenario:

Your school has been charged with building a back porch to encourage the activities rated in Step 1 of this exercise. Discuss the following points:

1. Who would you invite to build the back porch in your school? Why?

2. When would you meet? Why?

3. What would you want to talk about? Why?

4. Why would people want to go there?

5. What role should the principal play?

6. How would you know if the back-porch conversations made a difference to student and teacher learning?

ADDITIONAL RESOURCES

Web Sites

Teacher Leaders Network. http://www.teacherleaders.org.
Teachers Network Leadership Institute. http://www.teachersnetwork.org/tnli.

Publications

Barth, R. (1990). *Improving schools from within: Teachers, parents, and principals can make the difference.* San Francisco: Jossey-Bass.

Bolman, L. G., & Deal, T. E. (1994). *Becoming a teacher leader: From isolation to collaboration.* Thousand Oaks, CA: Corwin.

Crowther, F. (2009). *Developing teacher leaders: How teacher leadership enhances school success.* Thousand Oaks, CA: Corwin.

Dana, N. (2009). *Leading with passion and knowledge: The principal as action researcher.* Thousand Oaks, CA: Corwin.

Danielson, C. (2006). *Teacher leadership that strengthens professional practice.* Alexandria, VA: Association for Supervision and Curriculum Development.

Fullan, M. (2001). *Leading in a culture of change.* San Francisco: Jossey-Bass.

Katzenmeyer, M., & Moller, G. (1996). *Awakening the sleeping giant: Leadership development for teachers.* Thousand Oaks, CA: Corwin.

Lambert, L. (1998). *Building leadership capacity in schools.* Alexandria, VA: Association for Supervision and Curriculum Development.

Lambert, L. (2000). Framing reform for the new millennium: Leadership capacity in schools and districts. *CJEAP,14.* Retrieved December 11, 2009, from http://www.umanitoba.ca/publications/cjeap/articles/lambert.html.

Lieberman, A. (1995). *The work of restructuring schools: Building from the ground up.* New York: Teachers College Press.

Lieberman, A., & Miller, L. (1990). Restructuring schools: What matters and what works. *Phi Delta Kappan, 71*(10), 759–764.

Lieberman, A, & Miller, L. (1999). *Teachers: Transforming their world and work* (2nd ed.). New York: Teachers College Press.

Lieberman, A., & Miller, L. (2004). *Teacher leadership.* San Francisco, CA: Jossey-Bass.

Pellicer, I. O., & Anderson, L. W. (1995). *A handbook for teacher leaders.* Thousand Oaks, CA: Corwin.

Poetter, T. S., & Badiali, B. J. (2001). *Teacher leader.* Larchmont, NY: Eye on Education.

Sergiovanni, T. J. (2000). *The lifeworld of leadership: Creating culture, community, and personal meaning in our schools.* San Francisco: Jossey-Bass.

Sergiovanni, T. J., & Starrat, R. J. (2002). *Supervision: A redefinition.* Boston: McGraw-Hill.

Wasley, P. A. (1991). *Teachers who lead: The rhetoric of reform and the realities of practice.* New York: Teachers College Press.

Wasley, P. A. (1992). Working together: Teacher leadership and collaboration. In C. Livingston (Ed.), *Teacher leaders: Evolving roles* (pp. 21–55). Washington, DC: National Education Association.

Whitaker, T. (2003). *What great principals do differently: Fifteen things that matter most.* Larchmont, NY: Eye on Education.

3

Thinking Outside the Clock and Inside the Budget

How to Find Time and Money for Job–Embedded PD

Time is the coin of your life. It is the only coin you have, and only you can determine how it will be spent. Be careful lest you let other people spend it for you.

—Carl Sandburg, poet

The opening quote to this chapter inextricably links the concepts of time and money. The lack of these resources, either singly or together, is the most frequently cited deterrent to engaging in job-embedded professional development. In this chapter, we tackle this problem head-on to help you discover creative strategies you can employ to take charge of time and money, rather than letting others determine how they're spent for you. Let's start with the concept of time.

FINDING TIME

As we were preparing to write this book, we e-mailed several of our innovative teacher and administrator friends—colleagues from different school districts across the nation—asking them to share with us any ideas they had utilized in finding time and resources to engage in job-embedded professional development. One of our esteemed colleagues, Gail Ritchie, from Fairfax County Schools in Virginia, wrote back,

> I'm pretty sure I told you how much I love the proposed title of your new book, *Powerful Professional Development: Building Expertise Within the Four Walls of Your School*, but I don't think I told you that two years ago I gave the keynote speech at the International Conference of Teacher Research using time as my theme. It was a fun speech to write as I shared all the song titles, sayings, and metaphors there are about time. What does this have to do with your book, you're probably wondering at this point. Probably nothing, I just find it endlessly fascinating that time is such an issue for us—there never seems to be enough time for us to accomplish all that we want to accomplish. So we keep trying to find ways around that. (Personal communication, May 18, 2009)

Gail did two great things for us in this correspondence. First, in mentioning the creative speech she wrote, she sent us on our own journey exploring issues of time and money in music and literature, which led us to the powerful opening quote to this chapter (as well as others). Second, in her sharing that notions of time "probably have nothing to do with the writing of your book," she helped us realize just the opposite. As we had been corresponding with professionals across the nation, we realized that wonderful administrators and teachers across the nation were finding ways to make powerful job-embedded professional development happen—so it definitely was doable! Although one of the central themes of their communications was that time for meaningful professional development is definitely a major issue, these busy educators were coming up with solutions that we recognized should be shared with the readers of this book.

In preparing this chapter, we also read quite extensively and found the concept of time addressed in loads of publications—way more than we realized existed! With Gail's help, we recognized that the issue of time is, and always will be—well, timeless. Therefore, our approach to this chapter is to help you consider the ways you currently think about time (and money) and help you reconsider time and money in light of the possibilities for job-embedded professional development.

What Are Your Current Conceptions of Time?

Perhaps, the most important step related to time and professional development is simply acknowledging that time is a factor rather than pretending issues of time management don't exist, or as often happens, totally dismissing job-embedded professional development even when you know it will be good for you and your school because you think you just don't have the time. In many ways, job-embedded professional development is like exercise. When our own work and lives become ultra busy, we often give up exercise, lamenting that we just don't have the time or vowing that we will do it later when we can find more time. We ignore the reports on the news and in magazines that regularly remind us that exercising is an important ingredient for overall fitness and health, and we cringe at our annual physicals when our doctors ask us what we are doing for exercise.

At the start of this school year, we decided to make a change. Even though it was difficult for us to take the time to exercise, we made a commitment to join a gym and work out three days a week. We both found that we felt better and slept better. Even though exercise was dipping into three to four hours a week of our work time in the short run, we were more productive in the long run. Exercise rejuvenated us, and our hour break three days a week helped us to respond to work tasks more productively and efficiently when we returned.

Engagement in job-embedded professional development is just like that. Research tells us that teacher professional development is an important ingredient for the overall professional health of an educator and is key to student learning (Darling-Hammond, 1997a, 1999). Yet, many educators do not engage in the process because they just can't find the time. Even though it is difficult to take the time for job-embedded professional development, if you make a commitment to it and safeguard a little time each week to engage in the process, you'll feel better, make important educational decisions in a more informed, thoughtful way, and return to the never-ending demands of teaching and/or educational administration with the energy necessary to face the challenges of each school day. Roland Barth (2001b) informs us that one reason it is so difficult for school leaders to become learners is a lack of time, but he reminds us, "For principals, as for all of us, protesting a lack of time is another way of saying other things are more important and perhaps more comfortable" (p. 157).

The first step in finding time to engage in job-embedded professional development is acknowledging that lack of time will *always* be an issue that confronts educators (and all human beings) in all they do; and while you acknowledge time as a potential barrier to job-embedded learning, make a simultaneous commitment to engage in this important and necessary work.

Exercise 3.1 helps you and your colleagues begin taking stock of your current conceptions of time.

Exercise 3.1   Taking Stock of Your Current Conceptions of Time

Directions: Perhaps a good way to make this commitment is to take stock of your current conceptions of time as they relate to professional development. To do so, gather some colleagues who are also interested in making powerful job-embedded professional development an integral part of their professional lives.

Step 1: Copy and cut apart the collection of quotes about time that appear in Table 3.1 so that each member of your group has at least one quote. If you have more than twelve people to interact with around issues of time, quotes may be repeated.

Step 2: After each of your colleagues randomly selects a quote, ask him or her to flip the quote over and write a statement relating this quote to his or her feelings about teacher professional development.

Step 3: Once everyone has written a statement, have your colleagues get up and mingle to find a partner who received a different quote from the one they received. Once everyone has a partner, state that each pair should share their quotes with their partners as well as the way they related each quote to teacher professional development.

Step 4: Repeat this process two or three more times.

Step 5: Once everyone has shared their quotes and the meaning the quote holds for them with three or four different partners, have everyone sit down, and lead a discussion about time and its relationship to the ways professional development for teachers has been actualized in the past and what needs to be done in relationship to time issues for it to be actualized in more powerful ways in the future.

If you do not have a group of colleagues to engage with in this discussion, read through the different quotes we selected about time that appear in the following table, and think about each one of them in relationship to professional development yourself. Think about what you learned about time and your conceptions of time as a result of engaging in this activity.

Table 3.1   Time Quotes

Watches are so named as a reminder—if you don't watch carefully what you do with your time, it will slip away from you. —Drew Sirtors	Much may be done in those little shreds and patches of time which every day produces, and which most men throw away. —Charles Caleb Colton
Time is but the stream I go a-fishing in. —Henry David Thoreau	Day, n. A period of twenty-four hours, mostly misspent. —Ambrose Bierce
How long a minute is, depends on which side of the bathroom door you're on. —Zall's Second Law	If you want work well done, select a busy man—the other kind has no time. —Elbert Hubbard
Time is an equal opportunity employer. Each human being has exactly the same number of hours and minutes every day. Rich people can't buy more hours. Scientists can't invent new minutes. And you can't save time to spend it on another day. Even so, time is amazingly fair and forgiving. No matter how much time you've wasted in the past, you still have an entire tomorrow. —Denis Waitely	Time, the cradle of hope. . . . Wisdom walks before it, opportunity with it, and repentance behind it: he that has made it his friend will have little to fear from his enemies, but he that has made it his enemy will have little to hope from his friends. —Charles Caleb Colton
Time is what we want most, but . . . what we use worst. —William Penn	One must learn a different . . . sense of time, one that depends more on small amounts than big ones. —Sister Mary Paul
Time is a great teacher, but unfortunately it kills all its pupils. —Louis Hector Berlioz	You must have been warned against letting the golden hours slip by; but some of them are golden only because we let them slip by. —James Matthew Barrie

FINDING MONEY

In these tough financial times—in addition to scrutinizing conceptions of time—it's critical to take stock of money and its relation to PD. In a recent Webinar titled "Creating Effective Teacher Professional Development in Tough Economic Times," Anthony Rebora, managing editor of teacher magazine.org and the *Teacher Professional Development Sourcebook,* hosted Stephanie Hirsh, executive director of the National Staff Development Council, and Regis Shields, director of Education Resource Strategies, to discuss this topic. Hirsh and Shields framed the economic downturn as an opportunity for schools to reexamine their PD efforts. Smaller budgets mean increased scrutiny. Schools have no choice but to shed PD that doesn't have clear results, and they must take further advantage of resources that are already in place.

How Do You Currently Spend Money?

Of course, the first place to begin budget scrutiny is to assess how PD money is being spent in your district in the first place. In a related article to his Webinar titled "Reinventing Professional Development in Tough Times," Anthony Rebora (2009) quotes Ed Wilgus, a former district PD manager who is cofounder of Systemic Human Resource Solutions, as saying, "Any district hiring a consultant to come in for one day for $10,000 or $15,000—that's a waste of time and money" (Rebora, 2009). Imagine how a school or district might use $15,000 to purchase time for teachers to learn and work together. In essence, innovative schools and districts are recognizing ways to use their money to build the metaphorical back porch discussed in Chapter 2, which provides the space for job-embedded, collaborative learning to occur.

If you are a principal or teacher reading this book, you likely have no direct control or say over the way your district allocates PD money. So, what can you do if your district is still one of the many districts across the nation that spend the bulk of their PD budgets on the hiring of outside consultants and require principals and teachers to attend these one-shot wonders? First, you can gently share some of the most-recent writings and research on effective PD with personnel in your central office and school board. There is clear consensus that the one-shot workshop is ineffective in and of itself in leading to teacher learning and teacher change (Sparks, 1994, 1997; Wood & Killian, 1998; Wood & McQuarrie, 1999). Seeing this same message repeated over and over again in the literature may indeed provide the impetus for your central office to reconsider heavy investment in one-shot deals.

Second, you can apply your own knowledge of effective PD to the consultant workshops your district provides. There is nothing inherently bad about a knowledgeable consultant coming in to talk with teachers and principals about an innovation. In fact, sometimes this can be a fine way to garner knowledge for practice, defined in Chapter 1. (Recall *knowledge for practice* helps educators become informed about new educational practices and the research that has legitimized their worth.) The problem in many districts is that the consultant's workshop is the beginning and end of the PD experience, leaving *knowledge of practice* and *knowledge in practice* uncultivated.

While you might not have control over the ways your district spends money from its overarching PD budget, you do have control over what can be done locally at your school as a follow-up to a district workshop, utilizing some of the strategies presented in this book to help teachers translate what they learn in that workshop into their practice over the course of a school year. By employing some of the strategies discussed later in this book, such as book study and Webinars, you can help teachers build a back porch that facilitates their engagement in job-embedded PD. In this way, you will get the best "bang for your buck," receiving a better return on your monetary investment in outside expertise, either by extending the workshop experience or by replacing it with job-embedded alternatives.

Finally, it's important not to use lack of money as an excuse for not engaging in job-embedded PD. To inspire, we turn to a quote we found in our journey through what's been said in literature and music about time and money:

> Empty pockets never held anyone back. Only empty heads and empty hearts can do that.
>
> —Norman Vincent Peale (Conservapedia, 2009)

Although money is always a scarce resource in schools, creative educators have learned how to pool and explore existing funds to provide job-embedded PD within their school walls. Many principals are able to identify a variety of existing funds such as Title I, stimulus money, foundation, and state or federal grants that can be used to support job-embedded PD. Principal Lacy Redd explains,

> I have used Title I money to pay for learning-community time for teams. Each team has substitutes purchased to cover their classes during the year to attend a training session on their chosen topic for a few hours, then time, as a team, to put together a plan for implementation of the training. Follow-up meetings occur to discuss how the implementation is going. (Personal correspondence, May 15, 2009)

Another way to save money is to create inside expertise. Lacy adds,

> We have used teachers within our building or others within the district to cut down on consulting fees and travel expense. For example,

we have developed experts in several areas of technology and set up afternoon training sessions so that our teachers don't have to travel to be trained on technology applications. These teachers are then available in our school to coach and support the other teachers' implementation of the innovation. I've approached many things this way, making the use of a program optional until several people become experts and then slowly moving toward everyone using it with teacher coaches ready to help in our building. This saves money and allows for professional development to occur right here in our building. (Personal correspondence, May 15, 2009)

As you can see, empty pockets have not held back the teachers at Newberry Elementary School from engaging in powerful job-embedded professional learning.

HOW TO USE TIME AND MONEY CREATIVELY

As previously shared, we began research for this book by contacting outstanding colleagues across the country and asking them to share any thoughts they had about creative ways they were making time and finding resources for job-embedded teacher learning. In addition, we went on a quest to locate others' writings about how time and money have been used to facilitate professional development. We were overwhelmed with the number of fine ideas that existed and were being implemented across the nation, and we synthesized all of our readings and responses from exemplary practitioners into six categories that help to organize creative uses of time and money. These categories are restructured time, staff time, release time, purchased time, better-used time, and technology time.

Restructured Time

Restructured time refers to strategies for rearranging time within teachers' contracted school day. Some possibilities for restructured time include

- instituting early student release or late start for students (where students are sent home early or arrive later one day a week or month);
- adding more and regularly scheduled professional development days within the school calendar;
- providing teachers who work together a common planning time on a weekly basis;
- extending the school day on four days of the week and dismissing earlier on the fifth day;

- extracting time from the existing schedule by taking a few minutes from each period to create an extra planning period for teachers;
- trying block scheduling to provide longer periods of release time for teachers; and
- extending the school calendar to allow for a critical mass of professional development days at the beginning and end of the school year.

Staff Time

Staff time refers to strategies that alter the ways staff are utilized. Some possibilities for staff time include the following:

- Making better use of the adults in your building who are not teachers (i.e., paraprofessionals, college interns, parents, community volunteers, and administrators). All of these adults can be engaged with students on a regular basis in purposeful ways to free up teachers to meet with one another during the school day. An underutilized source is the adult volunteer. Create and train a volunteer pool that provides your school with more adults to disperse and utilize in creative ways to free teachers.
- Instituting "specialist days." Specialist days are full days where students rotate through their media, art, music, computer, and physical education specials for an entire day, freeing up time for classroom teachers to meet.

Release Time

Closely related to staff time, release time refers to strategies that "release" teachers during the contracted school day from other responsibilities so that they may engage in the work of job-embedded professional learning. Here are some possibilities for release time:

- Creating a bank of substitute hours that teachers can "cash in" to use for their professional development needs.
- Requiring all students to be involved in a certain number of community-service hours over the course of a school year; while students are out earning community service hours, teachers can meet.
- Hiring part-time permanent substitutes whose job is to rotate through the school releasing teachers when needed to attend to professional development needs. Permanent subs ensure that continuous learning occurs even when the teacher of record leaves the classroom. A great and underutilized source of permanent substitutes is retired educators. Recruit retired educators for your permanent substitute pool!
- Developing an intentional, systematic extracurricular event or activity provided by the community so that students engage in a wide

range of meaningful programs that supplement the curriculum while teachers work on school improvement.

- Creating partner classrooms by teaming different subject-area classes (in middle and high school) and different grade-level classrooms (in elementary school). Teachers in partner classrooms take turns taking responsibility for a designated amount of time for the other teacher's classroom (along with their own classroom), engaging in a meaningful curricular experience for the double-sized class of students.

A middle school example might be the language arts and science teachers' team. The language arts teachers take the double class and engage the whole group in a creative writing activity about mitosis, the topic currently being taught by the science teacher, while the science teachers are released to meet with each other. On the following week, the science teachers teach the double class, enacting the process of mitosis as a group dance, while the language arts teachers are released to meet with each other.

An elementary school example: The fifth-grade classrooms partner with the kindergarten classrooms. Each week, the kindergarten teachers and fifth-grade teachers alternate running a partner-reading program where fifth graders read to their kindergarten partner for thirty minutes right before lunch, freeing up either the fifth-grade or kindergarten team to meet an hour each week over lunch (thirty-minute reading time plus lunch time).

- Using large classes for special topics, creating independent study for students, or substituting appropriate television or video programming occasionally for regular instruction.

Purchased Time

Purchased time refers to providing incentives for teachers to spend time outside of the contractual day to engage in job-embedded professional development. Payment for this extra time can cover weekends, afterschool, and summer work and may be

- additional pay—a great way to reinvest some of the money a district can save by not relying on an expensive educational consultant;
- continuing certification hours—that is, hours needed for professional license renewal; or graduate credits if a district partners with a college of university;
- traded time—trading a Saturday workday and getting the day before Thanksgiving off; or
- traded requirements—for tenured teachers, trading participation in the annual observation, conference, and evaluation cycles with the administrator with a more meaningful production of a teacher-learning

portfolio that captures evidence related to the teachers and their students' growth over the course of the school year.

Better-Used Time

Better-used time refers to strategies for refocusing meeting times that are already in place but may not be currently utilized to their fullest potential. Such meeting times and their new agendas might include the following:

- Faculty meetings—rather than the administrator utilizing the bulk of this time to make announcements, the administrator takes care of announcements through e-mails and newsletters, and faculty meeting time is replaced with substantive professional development time utilizing some of the strategies for professional learning that appear in the next part of this book. For example, our colleague, principal Lacy Redd shares, "I have used faculty meetings once a month as school-improvement training opportunities, keeping all the 'sit and get info' to e-mails." Lacy elaborates, "Each faculty meeting has three foci, including new instructional approaches, technology updates, and one curriculum piece that is part of the overall school-improvement plan."
- Grade-level team meetings and department meetings (in elementary and middle schools, and high schools, respectively)—in many schools, the time during these meetings is taken up with congenial conversation or complaining. Congenial conversations refer to the friendly, cordial dialogue that some teachers have with one another in the workplace. We see congeniality when teachers chat about weekend plans, last night's football game, or the latest episode of *American Idol*. Although schools need congeniality, congeniality alone does not promote teacher learning and professional knowledge construction. Complaining sessions are times that teachers vent about difficulties they may be experiencing with individual students or classes or requirements from the school administration, district administration, or state. Although venting is sometimes a necessary release for the stresses associated with teaching, complaint sessions in and of themselves generally never solve issues or problems, and may even contribute to plummeting morale. Scrutinize the ways grade-level and department meeting time is currently being utilized in your school to assess if too much time is spent on congenial conversation in lieu of collegial learning or on conversation that gets stuck in a cycle of complaint. Work to replace congenial and complaint conversation time with some of the strategies in the second part of this book.
- Teacher workday—many districts have two to four professional development days scheduled into their school calendars throughout

the year; the students have a holiday while their teachers work. Often, these professional development days are used to host a one-shot workshop. Rather than fill all of these days with workshops, think about using the time for teachers to meet with one another to engage in lesson study, learning-community meetings, or book study—and at the end of a school year, to share the results of their job-embedded professional learning.

Technology Time

Technology time refers to the use of current technology to make it easier for teachers to meet and engage in professional discussion and learning. For example, it is often easier for teachers to meet and converse with one another in an asynchronous fashion than it is to meet face to face, as this provides teachers with flexibility in the ways they utilize their time. It is often also easier for teachers from different schools within the same district to meet virtually rather than face-to-face to save travel time. Asynchronous conversation and virtual meetings can be accomplished through online discussion forums, blogging, Twittering, and Facebook groups, and video conferencing.

Once again we return to our discussions with Lacy, and she explains,

As far as job-embedded professional development, we utilize blogs to do learning communities and book studies. I have found that people enjoy being able to post at anytime of day and not having to add a meeting to their busy schedules. It also doesn't require stipends to meet after school. Teachers get points toward recertification.

AN EXAMPLE: FINDING TIME AND MONEY FOR JOB-EMBEDDED PD

Technology isn't the only way to find time. Elementary principal Felicia Moss explains how she allocates time and resources to support the embedded professional learning community work within her school.

We have professional learning communities that meet every Wednesday afternoon except for the third Wednesday of each month, which is designated by the district as "District Professional Development Wednesday." We have student early release every Wednesday. Teachers use the time from 12:30 to 2:45 for professional development focused on our school-based needs.

The groups that meet on these Wednesday are formed in several ways. For example, we have preset communities at the beginning of the year by grade: PreK-1, Grades 2 and 3, and Grades 4 and 5. These groups developed out of our school plan. Teacher facilitators were also trained to facilitate these PLCs and to work with teachers to facilitate at various times. The topics of these PLCs came from questions, issues, and the interests of the communities, and also all three communities came together on schoolwide topics of interest.

At other times, we have what we call "Open PLC" where different research or issues are being studied, and teachers go to the one that they choose. These groups sometimes go on for weeks, sometimes only for a few sessions, based on the focus.

In addition, teachers are given time on every Thursday to work within their team or grade level on professional development using topics stemming from student work, data, or planning. Other teachers or the curriculum resource teacher, reading coach, counselor, behavior resource teacher, or the media specialist facilitate these groups as needed.

Teachers are encouraged to use inquiry as their professional development plan that is required by the state or district. Inquiry groups run throughout the year with a teacher volunteer and principal serving as facilitator. The principal also participated in inquiry and presented, along with seven teachers, at an end-of-the-year inquiry showcase. These teachers all used inquiry as their professional development plan, which is required by the state.

Teacher workdays or evenings are used as an opportunity for professional development. These days occur four times per year.

Sometimes, as the principal, I also provide coverage for teachers to visit other classroom on campus or at other schools. Subs are hired using money generated by fundraising initiatives, advanced placement funds, or paraprofessionals take over the classroom, often under the supervision of another teacher. The principal and support staff are also used to cover classes to allow teachers time to visit or to plan with other teachers.

Felicia Moss has found ways to provide time and garner resources for teachers to collaborate with each other in job-embedded ways that have led to enhanced teacher and student learning. Exercise 3.2 is designed to help you think about ways to find time in your school and district that can allow you to create a collaborative and powerful professional learning context.

Exercise 3.2   Scheduling Time Within the School Day

If Felicia can do it, so can you! With a team of teachers and administrators at your school, county office, or school board, revisit the various ways to capture time for professional learning. What are the real barriers to rethinking time management in your school? How can you and your team remove these barriers?

CONCLUDING THOUGHTS

As you can see, time and money are not insurmountable barriers. They just take a little rethinking within the school—and in some cases, persuading those who may not yet understand the importance of creating quality collaborative, professional learning time. This type of professional development is not cost free, but it is much more cost effective: That is, it is economical in terms of tangible benefits produced in teacher and student learning as a result of time and money spent.

As you near the completion of Part I of this text, we hope you have (1) developed an enhanced understanding of what job-embedded professional learning is and the types of building blocks needed to support this work, (2) applied the building blocks to the creation of a "back porch" in your school or district where conversations between teachers and administrators occur that support professional learning, and (3) identified ways to make time and find money to do this important work. You are now armed with a great deal of knowledge about job-embedded professional learning.

While knowledge is power, however, knowledge alone can't make this happen. In addition to knowledge, teachers must have the tools necessary to support the movement of new knowledge into practice. Part II will be devoted to helping you build that professional toolbox. Since a perceived lack of time and/or money presents such a great barrier to job-embedded, professional development efforts, be sure to pause and complete the final exercise in this chapter before moving on to Part II. This exercise will help you create the momentum needed to surmount time and money issues and utilize some of the many tools that lie ahead.

Exercise 3.3   How Do I Go About Incorporating Some of These Creative Time and Money Plans Into My Practice?

We hope that the ideas presented in the last section of this chapter got you thinking creatively about how you might implement some of these strategies as well as come up with your own uses of time and money to make job-embedded PD a reality in your school. To help you develop an action plan, end the reading of this chapter by engaging in the following exercise.

1. Read through all of the bulleted items suggesting creative uses of time introduced in the prior section ("How to Use Time and Money Creatively") of this chapter.

2. Place a check by bullets that indicate creative strategies you are already implementing.

3. Place an X next to the bulleted items you believe would be so difficult to implement in your context that they are not a good place to concentrate your initial efforts.

4. Place a circle around the remaining strategies that you believe hold promise for finding the time and resources necessary to begin or strengthen job-embedded PD in your school or district.

5. Reread each circled bulleted strategy. Place a star next to the strategy you believe to have the greatest potential to succeed in your context.

6. Create a to-do list of steps that need to be accomplished to actualize that strategy.

7. Do it!

ADDITIONAL RESOURCES

Davis, M. R. (2009, March 13). *Online professional development weighed as cost-saving tactic.* Retrieved December 3, 2009, from http://www.edweek.org/dd/articles/2009/03/13/04ddprofdev.h02.html.

Johnston, J., Knight, M., & Miller, L. (2007). Finding time for teams. *Journal of Staff Development, 28*(2), 14–18.

Khorsheed, K. (2007). Four places to dig deep to find more time for teacher collaboration. *Journal of Staff Development, 28*(2), 43–45.

Rebora, A. (2009). *Reinventing professional development in tough times.* Retrieved March 16, 2009, from http://www.teachermagazin.org/tsb/articles/2009/03/16/02pd_budget.

von Frank, V. (2008). *Finding time for professional learning.* Oxford, OH: National Staff Development Council.

PART II

The Professional Development Toolbox

*Strategies to Actualize
Powerful Professional Development*

Drawing by Shawn Black.

Chapters 4 through 10, in which we describe a number of strategies for strengthening teacher learning within your school walls, constitute a professional development toolbox from which you can select the most appropriate tools for your particular learning goals. Although we have witnessed these tools as successful in actualizing changes in teaching practice, they are just a sampling of the many professional learning tools available to educators interested in strengthening their teaching and students' learning.

As we introduce each of these professional development strategies, you will notice that many of them cultivate multiple professional knowledge building blocks introduced in Chapter 1 (Table 1.1). In planning powerful job-embedded learning, we are really trying to systematically and intentionally use the building blocks to carefully construct professional knowledge. As we put the blocks together, we must understand which tools are useful in creating each building block as well as the importance of planning professional development that moves across the building blocks, both horizontally and vertically. The goal is to account for each type of building block so that your professional development plan will be powerful enough to change instruction and strengthen student learning. Hence, we chose to introduce these tools in a progression, beginning with strategies that primarily encourage knowledge *for* practice and are relatively simple in design and structure, and proceed along a continuum in which the complexity of the strategies increases and are designed to develop knowledge *in* and *of* practice.

The tools in Chapter 4 are really opportunities to learn research-based practices and bring outside expertise into your building in less expensive ways than hiring a consultant to give a workshop or traveling to a professional conference. Here, we introduce book studies, Webinars, podcasts, and online video libraries. Although the learning from these tools cannot insure transfer to teaching practice, the type of knowledge created by tapping into this research is critical to improving schools. By learning from others, we are able to stand on the shoulders of giants who have inquired before us.

Recognizing that using the tools to create knowledge *for* practice is not enough to ensure effective implementation, in Chapters 5 and 6 we explore two tools that rely heavily on classroom observations and are a bit more sophisticated in their complexity: research-in-action and coteaching (Chapter 5). These tools allow teachers to view an innovation *in* practice. Next, three similar strategies, which we call conversation tools, are introduced to fill an important compartment in the professional development tool kit: protocols, open space technology, and knowledge cafés (Chapter 6). These tools highlight collaborative conversation and reflection, another vital building block to powerful professional learning.

Finally, in Chapters 7 through 10, we explore a number of highly complex and sophisticated tools that are powerful enough to develop knowledge *of* practice: lesson study (Chapter 7), action research or teacher inquiry (Chapter 8), coaching (Chapter 9), and learning communities

(Chapter 10). These learning-rich strategies, though they require more time and effort to implement, include every single building block to powerful professional learning described in Chapter 1.

Although we have tried to introduce these tools somewhat sequentially, this is not a neat and tidy process. As you move through Part II, you will note that each tool will often address multiple knowledge sources, knowledge types, orientations, and learning needs. Therefore, after we introduce, define, and illustrate each tool, we return to the Figure 1.1 we introduced in Chapter 1 that summarizes all of the building blocks of powerful professional learning, each time highlighting those building blocks that each particular tool addresses. The ultimate goal is to carefully and systematically select a tool or combination of tools to meet your professional learning purpose, a concept we'll more fully develop in Part III of this text.

Given that student learning relies on the quality of teacher learning, your job of creating powerful job-embedded, professional development opportunities for the teachers in your building is essential. Your success will depend in part upon becoming familiar with a number of tools (or professional development strategies) that can help you accomplish this task. By the time you finish Part II, you will be knowledgeable about a variety of different tools that can be utilized at various times and in various combinations to meet the professional learning demands within your school walls. As we explore each tool, be sure to consider the following:

- How can that tool be used to plan for the required knowledge source, type, orientation, and learning needs?
- How might this tool be used for group, dyad, or individual learning?
- What type of data might you collect while using that tool?
- What is your degree of comfort and familiarity with the tool?
- How ready is your school's culture to implement the tool?
- How would you carve out time to use that tool in your building?
- What resources would you need to successfully use this tool?

Part II of this book is designed to provide you with a good start on creating your own professional development toolkit. After reading Chapters 4 through 10 and considering the questions we posed above, you will be able to

1. describe a variety of job-embedded, research-based professional development tools to other professionals;

2. identify tools that would support the development of knowledge for, in, and of practice for a job-embedded professional development need at your school; and

3. conduct a needs assessment of the resources that you would need to implement each tool at your school.

4

Book Studies, Webinars, Podcasts, and Online Video Libraries

Our school's book studies provide a forum for teachers to focus on a topic, build knowledge, share thoughts, and make decisions about how they can introduce new ideas to their classrooms. However, the most powerful action that I have seen come out of book studies is the forging of relationships between teachers from different grade levels, different hallways, as well as with our leadership team. A great book study creates conversations and develops a shared professional vocabulary! Most important, our book club's writing conversations set the stage for transforming instruction at our school. Although it was just the beginning, the book study set our school on the road to becoming a true learning community.

—Jessica Jones-Cummings, Jackson Elementary Principal

The podcasts worked perfectly for teachers' schedules. They are flexible. Our school has a lot of young teachers with young children. We often feel pressed to leave as soon as the contract day has ended. I know that none of us stop working when we go home. I grade papers when my kids are playing in the backyard or while I am at the ball game. But when the kids go to bed, I can listen to the podcasts, create a trial lesson plan and assessment tool, and then I am ready to discuss the work presented on the podcast and some of my ideas with my colleagues either in an online wiki or blog from home or in our PLC when I get back to school.

—Jackie Polly, Martin Elementary Teacher

The Webinars are great because we don't have to travel all over the country to hear about new ideas. They bring new ideas to me and are also interactive so that we can get clarification right away. Although they aren't as flexible as podcasts, they are typically offered multiple times, which allows for greater participation.

—Yolanda Hall, Germantown Elementary Teacher

Our school just purchased PD 360 this year. We love it for our professional learning communities. This is basically a video library that gives us flexible access to research-based practices in a timely and convenient format. Once our learning community has looked at our student data to define a dilemma of practice, we turn to PD 360 to explore possible solutions. The teachers love this as they can use it both individually and collaboratively. By discussing what they viewed, we begin to create a shared understanding of research-based practice.

—Milton Shank, Citrus County Assistant Superintendent

Jessica, Jackie, Yolanda, and Milton are each offering unique insight into the power and flexibility of the first four professional development tools that we will place in our toolkit. In their own words, they describe these tools as helping teachers focus on a topic, build knowledge, share thoughts, make decisions, forge professional relationships, create conversations, develop shared professional vocabulary, build shared understandings, set the stage for transforming instruction, and explore possible solutions to a school's felt difficulty.

In this chapter, we have grouped book studies, Webinars, podcasts, and online video libraries together because these tools provide flexible and powerful opportunities for educators to learn new knowledge from outside sources without hiring an expensive speaker, providing substitutes, or sending large numbers of faculty to lengthy conferences. Although these four tools possess many similarities, the tools do vary in their delivery and can accommodate both individual and collaborative reflection. In order to help you understand the nuances of these tools, we define each of the tools and then provide an illustration of how a school might utilize them to strengthen knowledge *for* practice.

DEFINITION: BOOK STUDY

As indicated in Jessica's quote, a book study provides external or outside professional knowledge to teachers. The book study offers educators a tool that can help them explore and prepare to implement new teaching practices in their classrooms. Book studies promote conversations among teachers leading to the application of new knowledge in classrooms powerful enough to improve existing professional skills as well as lead to school change and community building. Book studies are relatively inexpensive and, typically, most enjoyable for educators when time is carved out to allow participation, and when a relevant book is selected.

DEFINITIONS: WEBINAR, PODCAST, AND ONLINE VIDEO LIBRARY

Jackie, Yolanda, and Milton provide great examples of why online professional development tools, such as Webinars, podcasts, and video libraries, can be effective ways to support teacher learning. Like book studies, these professional development tools allow educators to learn about the latest research, but in an online, interactive environment rather than through the shared reading of a printed publication. Many professional organizations offer Webinars (or seminars over the Web) where experts deliver professional information, and teachers are invited to interact with the speakers in an online environment. Another convenience of Webinars is that they are often archived and can be revisited at a later date by teachers who were unavailable for the initial Webinar broadcast.

Podcasts are also online tools: audio or video presentations that can be accessed on demand. By accessing podcasts, teachers across your school and district can "click into" timely and helpful professional development sessions tied to school goals and learning needs. Podcasts can be developed by people inside the district, or you can select podcasts from outside providers that target your district or school's unique needs. Since podcasts are not synchronous, they can be accessed "24/7" based on the teacher's schedule. They can be listened to anywhere and at anytime!

Video libraries are similar to podcasts in that they are available on demand and are not interactive. For example, the PD 360 Web site (which can be found at http://www.schoolimprovement.com/pd360-info.cfm) is an example of an online library that serves as a robust professional development tool for teachers and administrators interested in hearing about and viewing current innovations in education.

School districts can purchase video library subscriptions for their teachers to use on demand. For example, the PD 360 Web site provides over two hundred hours of research-based video content, plus tools for follow-up, tracking, reflection, and group training. Well-known educational leaders, including Rick Stiggins, Rick DuFour, and Michael Fullan, offer video segments about research-based innovation on PD 360. Additionally, the speaker segments are complemented by over three thousand classroom examples that allow educators to witness the implementation of best practices. One superintendent from a rural school district that we work with explained,

> PD 360 is one of the most comprehensive solutions ever offered to rural schools. It gives those closest to our children—teachers, administrators, aspiring leaders, coaches, mentors, paraprofessionals, and professional learning communities—access to innovation without leaving the school building.

ILLUSTRATION: FROM BOOK STUDY TO WEBINAR AND BACK AGAIN

Our illustration of these knowledge-for-practice tools begins with a book study focused on improving writing instruction at Jackson Elementary School where Jessica Jones-Cumming sought to lead writing reform. Let's listen to Jessica reflect on the writing-reform effort that began at Jackson Elementary with the book study.

A Book Study

Jessica begins,

> We were quite excited when fourteen people decided to join the Jackson Elementary Book Study. Our group was an eclectic combination of educators. Included was the principal, reading coach, special educators, across-grade-level representation of classroom teachers, doctoral students interested in literacy from the university, and a university faculty member interested in writing instruction. The group came together in person and electronically to discuss *The Art of Teaching Writing* by Lucy Calkins. We had named writing reform as an important need based on an analysis of our test scores.

As we began eavesdropping on the first meeting the group held to discuss the book, we heard the teachers wrestling with the tension between creating writers and creating students who can score high on the state writing exam. One teacher began,

> I feel that Lucy Calkins teaches writing the *whole-language* way. The FCAT [Florida Comprehensive Achievement Test] wants children to

be masters of writing by fourth grade. I find the pressure from the FCAT to be a negative factor in allowing me to teach the way Lucy outlines in the book. I do believe in what she is advocating though.

Another teacher continues,

Calkins talks about writing as accomplished through a sophisti-cated collection of skills that we cultivate as we scaffold children's writing development. I really think we are currently pushing children to build a writing skill set that is only one block wide and several blocks high. Many children can do it, but only our best writers have a wide base of support for the upper blocks that FCAT tests. We are short changing the average writers.

The conversation continues,

Writing isn't just learning a technique, either. Calkins lays out writing as a developmental process that successful children go through that allows them to build a strong writing base.

Another teacher chimes in,

We are really looking at how to teach children to think, and then how to express that thought! This gets to the heart of what we want to accomplish in the classroom anyway. I am looking to incorporate more thoughtful listening and speaking activities, like those discussed in the book.

This first book-study meeting ended with the group members deciding on which chapters they will read during the next week, and they all head home. The next meeting begins with one teacher sharing her understanding of Lucy Calkin's entire approach to writing, which ignites the discussion that afternoon. One teacher responds,

You hit the target, Julie! Your description of the entire process is just how it works. As far as being fully present as a listener, I find being a listener one of the most enjoyable parts of teaching writing. As I look into the earnest, tentative eyes of a young writer, I realize the enormous risk they take each time they share their writing with me. It would be unthinkable to impose my own value judgments on the quality of their words. And yet, as teachers, we are required to do just that. The fine line, as Calkins so aptly describes, is how to do it with care and respect for the author.

In this illustration, you can see the teachers building a new and shared knowledge of what it means to be a writer and teacher of writing. The group collaboratively wrestles with the tensions they feel as they contemplate infusing a "Lucy Calkins" approach to writing within a context of high-stakes accountability.

A Webinar

After the book study ends, Jessica contemplates how she will bring the larger teaching force from her school into the writing conversation. Her initial book-study team members are positioned to serve as teacher leaders. Jessica rallies the original members of the book-study team to decide on next steps. Together, they believe they can get whole-faculty involvement in focusing on writing instruction by forming learning teams, each led by one member of the original book-study group. To plan and prepare to do so, the book-study group members participate in a free Webinar offered by *Teacher Magazine* featuring Nancy and another educator, Anne Jolly. As they read the following description of the Webinar, the group believes it would be extremely valuable to help them with the next steps in their work:

> In this webinar, Anne Jolly and Nancy Fichtman Dana will explain how to create the framework and establish ground rules for building successful professional learning teams. Together, they will answer questions on how you can form powerful and productive professional learning teams at your school. (Jolly & Dana, 2009)

Professional learning teams are small groups of educators working together at a school to improve instruction and learning. They are quickly gaining prominence as a model for teacher professional development. At their best, they offer educators onsite, research-based, embedded training with the shared objective of advancing student learning.

Some of the teachers gathered in one of the classrooms after school to watch the one-hour Webinar. One of the them watched the Webinar from her home, and another viewed the archived version of the Webinar a few weeks later. By the time the team met again, each teacher understood the purpose of professional learning teams, and they set out to deepen the entire Jackson Elementary faculty's understanding of writing instruction by formulating these teams.

Back to a Book Study, Online

Interestingly, the first whole-faculty activity within the newly formed professional learning teams was to develop their faculty's interest in creating change in writing instruction. Each teacher was provided with Lucy Calkin's book, and they began an online book study using a simple blog as the conversation tool. The learning-team facilitator (one of the original book-study group members) provided a discussion prompt for each chapter, and then the group logged on asynchronously to respond and discuss with each other.

The professional learning teams also logged into PD 360 during a variety of meetings to watch a series of writing-related videos that would help strengthen their understanding of the writing knowledge base. Much like the book study, the video library provided new information that generated teacher discussion.

WHAT HAVE WE LEARNED?

Table 4.1 illustrates that these four professional development tools primarily help teachers create knowledge *for* practice by cultivating an understanding of research-based practice from outside sources. In addition, these tools can develop all six types of knowledge—pedagogical, curricular, content, context, pedagogical content, or student knowledge— depending on the topic of the book selected and a group's identified need. Some of the benefits of these four tools include expanding the participants' understanding of the research base of teaching, encouraging innovation, and building collegiality through shared discussions.

Although these four tools share the purpose of strengthening teacher knowledge from external sources, the tools vary in their *type of delivery* and can be used for both *individual* and *collaborative* reflection. When choosing book studies, Webinars, podcasts, and online video libraries as your professional development tools, you are recognizing that important knowledge is available outside of your school and that you can strengthen teaching, learning, and relationships by exploring these sources together. This type of knowledge is important as we can then stand on the shoulders of giants rather than reinvent the knowledge wheel. As you witnessed in the illustration of writing reform at Jackson Elementary, within the first few months of school, this school-reform effort generated interest in and attention to writing across the entire teaching staff.

SOME THINGS TO THINK ABOUT

As illustrated, these four tools can strengthen knowledge for practice. However, just as a carpenter checks out his tools and organizes his workshop before beginning his project, those of us planning professional development must be sure our context is ready for the professional learning we are hoping to accomplish. For these reasons, we need to consider the following questions and plan ahead.

Table 4.1 Book Studies, Podcasts, Webinars, and Online Libraries: Building Blocks for Powerful Professional Learning

Building-Block Type	*Building Blocks*						*Theorists*
Learning Needs	Understanding of research-based practice	View model	Practice time	Feedback and coaching	Collaborative conversation and reflection		Borko (2004); Desimone (2009); Joyce and Showers (1983)
Orientation	Outside orientation			Inside orientation			Marzano, Pickering, and Pollock (2001); Cochran-Smith and Lytle (1999, 2001, 2009)
Type of Knowledge	Pedagogical knowledge	Curriculum knowledge	Student knowledge	Content knowledge	Context knowledge	Pedagogical content knowledge	Grossman (1990); Magnusson, Krajcik, and Borko (1999); Shulman (1987a, 1987b)
Source of Knowledge	Knowledge for practice		Knowledge in practice		Knowledge of practice		Cochran-Smith and Lytle (1999, 2001, 2009)

• *What is the degree of comfort and familiarity with the tool?*

Although book studies are more familiar to teachers, feeling comfortable with using the technology associated with an online library, Webinars, book-study discussion blogs, and podcasts will be critical to gaining participation. Initial resistance often exists as online learning tools are introduced and integrated into teacher professional learning. However, you can ease that unrest by providing convenient access to technology, time for teachers to become comfortable with the technology, and "just in time" coaching for teachers as they begin using the new tools.

• *How ready is your school's culture to implement these tools?*

When introducing book studies, podcasts, Webinars, and online libraries, we need to create a reason or urgency that stimulates teachers' interest in learning. Often, this comes from involving teachers in reviewing student data and establishing strategic goals for their school, grade level, and classroom. In addition to being motivated to learn, the participants must possess an openness to knowledge constructed outside their local context, and they must be willing to explore innovation introduced by external sources that may sometimes conflict with their existing beliefs and practices.

• *How would you carve out time to use these tools?*

Although book studies, podcasts, Webinars, and online libraries are flexible tools that allow teachers to learn both inside and outside the school day, each tool still requires the teacher make a time commitment. Some ways to encourage teachers to make the time commitment to these initial stages of professional learning is to tie their evaluation goals to building this new knowledge, offering professional development credit for participation, or even encouraging participation as a part of National Board activities.

• *What resources would you need to successfully use this tool?*

Successful implementation of these four professional development tools will require leaders within schools to have access to financial, physical, and human resources. For example, books and subscriptions need to be purchased. Computers must be available and functioning. Internet must be in good working order and Web sites can't be blocked. Technology support must be within reach. By thinking carefully about the resources needed prior to introducing the professional development tool, we are much more likely to be successful.

- *What type of data might you collect while using these tools?*

Given that knowledge for practice is a "stage setting" activity for generating interest in new research-based innovations that could transform classroom practice, collecting data that demonstrates the impact of these four tools will rely mostly on self-report measures and analysis of teacher conversations. Asking teachers to summarize what they have learned as a result of participating in a book study, Webinar, podcast, or using an online library is an easy way to capture current understandings.

As you plan to cultivate knowledge for practice within your school, remember to consider these questions. By taking the time to create readiness; providing the necessary human, financial, and physical resources; as well as creating a data-collection plan to see if your professional learning time yielded results, you are setting the stage for successful professional learning.

ADDITIONAL RESOURCES

Webinar, Podcasts, and Video Library Examples

Annenberg Media. http://www.learner.org.
Edutopia Podcasts. http://www.edutopia.org/video.
Folger Shakespeare Library. http://www.folger.edu/template.cfm?cid=2936.
PBS Teachers Live. http://www.pbs.org/teachers/webinar.
PD 360 Online Video Library. http://www.schoolimprovement.com/pd360-info.cfm.

Publications

Borthwick, A., & Pierson, M. (Eds.). (2008). *Transforming classroom practice: Professional development strategies.* Eugene, OR: International Society for Technology in Education.

Keller, B. (2008). Hitting the books. *Education Week, 02*(01), 4, 6. http://www.edweek.org/tsb/articles/2008/09/10/01books.h02.html.

5

Research-in-Action and Coteaching

Research-in-action was great! We not only received information but we also experienced hands-on and minds-on activities and observed real teachers doing what we just learned about! What we saw today was practical learning that can be transferred to our own teaching. We saw students doing science and fully engaged in learning through inquiry. Thanks! You have expanded my horizons!

—Research-in-Action Day Feedback Form,
P. K. Yonge Developmental Research School

Coteaching is a promising and cost-effective tool that is applicable to almost any teaching situation. When we carefully paired teachers, we provided daily classroom support for them to collaboratively explore and implement new instructional innovations. This works really well when we have a more experienced teacher paired with a less experienced teacher.

—Carolyn Blackshere, Martin Luther King Principal

These educators' insights recognize the power and flexibility of our next two professional development tools, research-in-action and coteaching. In their words, these tools provide hands-on and minds-on scaffolded learning through observation, identify ways to integrate new knowledge into teaching, collaboratively explore and implement new instructional innovations, and identify possible solutions to a school's felt difficulty.

In this chapter, we have grouped research-in-action and coteaching together as these tools both rely heavily on the powerful role observation of teaching colleagues can play in professional learning. In addition, for both of these strategies, the professional learning context is the classroom. Although these two tools both incorporate classroom observation, the tools do vary in their type of delivery. In order to help you understand the nuances of these tools, we define and illustrate each of the tools to demonstrate how a school might utilize them to assure a deep understanding of knowledge *for* practice as well as provide a window through which to begin creating knowledge *in* practice.

DEFINITION: RESEARCH-IN-ACTION

Research-in-action (RIA) is an innovative knowledge-for-practice professional development strategy that goes a step further than the strategies discussed in the previous chapter. To deepen understanding of the theoretical and conceptual underpinnings as well as the nuts and bolts of implementation, teacher teams visit a school site where the practice they are interested in bringing to their school is currently being widely implemented. The day-long school visit consists of three parts: (1) attending a seminar on the innovation, (2) observing the targeted research-based practice as it is unfolding in the classrooms in that school, and (3) debriefing with those teachers whom they observed after the students are dismissed. The version of RIA we share with you was created by the administrators and faculty at the P. K. Yonge Developmental Research School in Gainesville, Florida, led by P. K. Yonge director Fran Vandiver and faculty member Lynda Hayes, but you can adapt this model to meet the needs of your school or district. In fact, a RIA day can occur within a single school if there are two or more teachers who are implementing an innovation that other teachers in the same school wish to learn about.

ILLUSTRATION: RESEARCH-IN-ACTION

P. K. Yonge serves as a laboratory school for the University of Florida. As such, it is a school committed to improving their own teaching by studying their implementation of research-based practices as well as tying research to demonstration in a way that supports teacher development both inside and outside the school. Hence, P. K. Yonge faculty developed a model of professional development that would cultivate important knowledge-for-practice opportunities that honor the age old teacher request, "Let me see it in action, and then I can do it."

A RIA day begins as visiting educators, consisting of a principal and teacher team from different schools interested in observing a particular innovation, meet in the P. K. Yonge campus community room. At that time, an administrator or faculty member provides an overview of the research-based practice and an immersion in the basic essentials of the instructional strategy being explored. For example, Dr. Rose Pringle, a University of Florida science educator who works closely with the school, introduces the concept of inquiry-based science to the group by engaging them in discussion of the theoretical foundations of the innovation, providing the group a demonstration of the approach, offering an experience using inquiry-based science, and then debriefing the work by collaboratively reviewing a video. This portion of the day provides an intense "under the microscope" view of this new teaching method that the visitors are about to observe.

After Dr. Pringle concludes the opening presentation and discussion, the teams move about the school and observe a variety of classrooms engaged in using the inquiry-based science approach. The classroom observers use specifically developed protocols to guide their observations. These protocols help to focus their gaze on important content and instructional and classroom-management issues related to teaching inquiry-oriented science. During the day, the school teams are able to observe the innovation at multiple grade levels and also witness how teachers with differing classroom styles are able to implement this science practice.

At the end of the day, the educators come together to debrief with the P. K. Yonge host teachers as well as administrators. This opportunity provides a time for reflection on the observations as well as an opportunity for the teams to ask logistical questions related to implementation and garnering the necessary resources and knowledge base to make the innovation successful when they return to their own schools. The ability to meet with those who have successfully implemented the science innovation provides a much-needed foundation for each school team. By the end of the day, the visiting classroom teachers and building leaders feel prepared to think more deeply about their current instruction as well as implement their new inquiry-based science knowledge.

DEFINITION: COTEACHING

Coteaching also provides teachers the opportunity to observe successful instruction modeled in the classroom. Coteaching is the practice of two teachers sharing responsibility for both teaching and learning as they collaboratively plan and deliver lessons, determine in advance the role each will play in the lesson, and reflect together on the teaching and learning that took place after the lesson is completed. Coteaching can take two forms—lead and support and parallel teaching. The lead-and-support approach is characterized by two teachers engaged together in planning and delivering the same lesson, with one teacher providing the primary instruction and the other teacher circulating and supporting. The parallel-teaching approach is characterized by two teachers dividing one class in half and each delivering the same lesson to a smaller group of students within the same classroom. In both approaches, by working side by side, coteaching allows teachers to share professional knowledge.

Borrowing from the inclusion literature, Wolff-Michael Roth and his colleagues (1999), as well as Bernard Badiali and Donna Hammond (2005), have developed coteaching as an alternative professional learning tool to the traditional student-teaching practice. During coteaching, the student teacher and master teacher share responsibility for all parts of the class rather than the typical observation followed by turning the class over to let the novice sink or swim. Today, coteaching has also become a part of inservice teacher professional development as teachers are paired to support each other's learning. Practicing teachers sometimes choose coteaching when one teacher has developed a beginning level of understanding and comfort with a new practice and is ready to try the practice with support. Coteaching can also be used as experienced teachers share instructional successes with each other.

ILLUSTRATION: COTEACHING— LEAD AND SUPPORT

Our illustration of coteaching as a tool for developing knowledge for and in practice begins as we watch the collaboration between Robert, a National Board–certified teacher with a successful career as an innovative writing teacher, and Jack, a teacher who just recently moved into the high school English department after spending years as an English-as-second-language (ESL) teacher.

While their backgrounds varied, Jack and Robert wanted to strengthen the quality of student writing in their composition classes. After spending five years helping students prepare for the state writing exam, they realized that the students had not developed their own voices as writers. Robert had recently become involved in the National Writing Project and was anxious to try out writers' workshop while Jack was particularly concerned about making sure he provided the instruction his students deserved, as he had spent most of his career working with ESL learners and was new to teaching English.

Hence, in an effort to strengthen Jack's instruction, Robert and Jack decided to coteach two sections of English by combining their third- and sixth-period classes. Fortunately, they taught in adjoining rooms that were separated by a folding door. The arrangement of their physical space allowed them to easily combine their classes by opening the divider for third and sixth period. In the beginning, Robert led and Jack offered assistance and support within the lesson. The power of coteaching within the lead-and-support model emerged as Robert took the lead in planning while Jack observed and supported the implementation of the planned lesson. As Jack began feeling more confident with the content, he began coplanning with Robert, which allowed Jack to ask questions about details of the lesson design and implementation. Over time, Jack became much more confident with the writers' workshop approach and began to collect student work that showed evidence that the class was embracing and demonstrating "voice" in their writing. As a result, Jack began to assume the lead-teacher role to test out his newly formed professional knowledge while Robert was still there to offer support.

ILLUSTRATION: COTEACHING— PARALLEL TEACHING

Our second illustration of coteaching as a tool for developing knowledge for and in practice occurs as we watch a parallel-teaching collaboration between Janey and Jessica. Parallel teaching offered Janey the opportunity to partner with another science teacher at her urban middle school. Janey was known as an exceptionally motivating teacher with strong classroom-management skills and a keen understanding of middle school students. Jessica, her coteacher, entered teaching through an alternative route from a career as a scientist. As such, she possessed deep content knowledge but knew she had a lot to learn about how to teach science. To support Jessica in her first year teaching, the principal assigned both Janey and Jessica to the same first-period class.

Janey and Jessica met each week to collaboratively plan the week's lessons. Given that parallel teaching offered Janey and Jessica the opportunity to jointly plan instruction, their planning capitalized on each teacher's unique expertise and provided the opportunity for them to learn from each other. Jessica would share her content expertise, and Janey would help her think about how to adapt that content to the middle school classroom and organize the environment for learning. In combination, they created lessons that were both content and instructionally rich.

Additionally, parallel teaching allowed each teacher to deliver the same lesson to half the class, which allowed Jessica to begin working with a smaller group of students. This provided Jessica opportunities to develop her classroom-management abilities without the challenges inherent in whole-class instruction. Janey explains after reflecting on her year, "Parallel teaching requires us to find joint planning time to ensure that we deliver robust content in the same way within our groups. The best part of this is that we learn together, before, during, and after teaching."

WHAT HAVE WE LEARNED?

Tables 5.1 and 5.2 illustrate the ways RIA and coteaching begin to move beyond the foundational knowledge-for-practice building blocks that are present in book study, Webinars, podcasts, and online library tools as RIA and coteaching provide teachers opportunities to observe the complexity of a teaching practice, hear how other teachers respond to the complexity of the practice, and collaboratively reflect in a way that begins to blur the boundaries of outside and inside professional knowledge. Also similar to the tools presented in Chapter 4, educators can use research-in-action and coteaching to develop all types of knowledge—pedagogical, curricular, content, context, and student knowledge—as teachers reflect on either what they have observed or what they have taught.

RIA and coteaching provide the opportunity for teachers to begin understanding how they can transfer what they are observing to the classroom. As such, in Tables 5.1 and 5.2 we see movement from knowledge-for-practice to knowledge-in-practice building blocks as well as movement from outside to inside orientations. These two tools vary in that the learning is through *observing* in research-in-action where learning is through both *observing* and *teaching* in coteaching. Hence, we see that teachers not only get to view a model in RIA days (an important professional development building block) but also get practice time in the coteaching strategy. Both of the tools encourage *collaborative* reflection on the teaching episode. When choosing RIA or coteaching as a professional development tool, you are recognizing that other teachers possess important knowledge that can improve other teachers' instruction.

SOME THINGS TO THINK ABOUT

- *What is the degree of comfort that exists with these tools at your school?*

Key to both research-in-action and coteaching is the teacher's openness to learning from teaching colleagues as well as a readiness to ask specific questions and share challenges with others. More specifically, RIA will require that teachers be comfortable being observed and making their teaching public to other teachers whether inside or outside their school. Coteaching allows the experienced instructor to set up an instructional episode that is known to work in the particular classroom, and this gives the other teacher a place to practice while minimizing the problems that can arise. Due to the isolated nature of the classroom, teachers are often uncomfortable and afraid of making mistakes in front of their colleagues. Finding the right teacher pairs is important to the success of coteaching. Coteaching will require teachers who are ready to share and comfortable with sharing all aspects of their classroom with another educator as well as recognizing that each teacher can learn from the other.

Table 5.1 Research-in-Action: Building Blocks for Powerful Professional Learning

Building-Block Type	Building Blocks						Theorists
Learning Needs	Understanding of research-based practice	View model	Practice time	Feedback and coaching	Collaborative conversation and reflection		Borko (2004); Desimone (2009); Joyce and Showers (1983)
Orientation	Outside orientation			Inside orientation			Marzano, Pickering, and Pollock (2001); Cochran-Smith and Lytle (1999, 2001, 2009)
Type of Knowledge	Pedagogical knowledge	Curriculum knowledge	Student knowledge	Content knowledge	Context knowledge	Pedagogical content knowledge	Grossman (1990); Magnusson, Krajcik, and Borko (1999); Shulman (1987a, 1987b)
Source of Knowledge	Knowledge for practice		Knowledge in practice		Knowledge of practice		Cochran-Smith and Lytle (1999, 2001, 2009)

Table 5.2 Coteaching: Building Blocks for Powerful Professional Learning

Building-Block Type	Building Blocks						Theorists
Learning Needs	Understanding of research-based practice		View model	Practice time	Feedback and coaching	Collaborative conversation and reflection	Borko (2004); Desimone (2009); Joyce and Showers (1983)
Orientation	Outside orientation			Inside orientation			Marzano, Pickering, and Pollock (2001); Cochran-Smith and Lytle (1999, 2001, 2009)
Type of Knowledge	Pedagogical knowledge	Curriculum knowledge	Student knowledge	Content knowledge	Context knowledge	Pedagogical content knowledge	Grossman (1990); Magnusson, Krajcik, and Borko (1999); Shulman (1987a, 1987b)
Source of Knowledge	Knowledge for practice		Knowledge in practice		Knowledge of practice		Cochran-Smith and Lytle (1999, 2001, 2009)

• *How ready is your school's culture to implement the tool?*

Most important to the success of these two strategies will be a culture of collaboration within the school. Implementing research-in-action within your school will require a different readiness level than visiting another school to study an innovation. In a competitive rather than collaborative school culture, when a teacher or group of teachers from a school are used to demonstrate model lessons, they will likely experience resistance. Similarly, coteaching in some classrooms and not others must be conceived of as a learning opportunity available to all so that competition for scarce resources dedicated to coteaching does not emerge.

• *How would you carve out time to use these tools in your building?*

Coteaching is actually one of the easiest tools for embedding into the school day as long as you have common planning time, since planning, teaching, and reflection can occur organically as teachers work side by side. RIA will still require teachers to leave the classroom to observe during the instructional day. Thus, the ideas presented in Chapter 3 can help identify ways to carve out time using your school's unique resources.

• *What resources would you need to successfully use these tools?*

Given that the knowledge being shared is that of accomplished teachers, the most important resources needed for successfully implementing RIA or coteaching are human resources. Finding and rewarding educators who are willing to embrace, implement, study, and make public to others their learning is essential. The learning generated through these tools is directly tied to the quality of the teacher knowledge being shared.

• *What type of data might you collect while using these tools?*

Both of these tools provide access to multiple types of data. For example, RIA generates student data in the form of student work that the observing teachers can review after the observation. Additionally, upon conclusion of the observation, teachers should be asked to provide a reflection on the day that specifies what they have learned and how their beliefs and practices may have shifted as a result of their new familiarity with the practice modeled. Coteaching naturally integrates the collection and discussion of data into the fabric of their shared work. As teachers collaboratively plan, teach, and assess their students, they have access to artifacts, dialogue, and student work that can help the coteaching team understand the degree of student learning accomplished. Coteaching discussions can also help teachers articulate new learning as well as future questions.

ADDITIONAL RESOURCES

Web Site

P. K. Yonge Developmental Research School, Research in Action Days. http://education.ufl.edu/grants/letas/development/ria.html.

Publications

Badiali, B., & Hammond, D. J. (2005). Co-teaching as an alternative to the "takeover" phenomenon. *Pennsylvania Teacher Educator, 4,* 32–41.

Conderman, G., Vresnahan, V., & Pedersen, T. (2008). *Purposeful co-teaching: Real cases and effective strategies.* Thousand Oaks, CA: Corwin.

Friend, M., & Cook, L. (2003). *Interactions: Coprofessionals* (4th ed.). Boston: Allyn and Bacon.

Roth, W.- M., Masciotra, D., & Boyd, N. (1999). Becoming-in-the-classroom: A case study of teacher development through co-teaching. *Teaching and Teacher Education, 15,* 771–784.

Tobin, K., Roth, W.- M., & Zimmerman, A. (2001). Learning to teach science in urban schools. *Journal of Research in Science Teaching, 38,* 941–964.

Villa, R. A., Thousand, J. S., & Nevin, A. I. (2008). *A guide to co-teaching: A multimedia kit for professional development* (2nd ed.). Thousand Oaks, CA: Corwin.

6

Conversation Tools

Protocols, Open–Space Technology, and the Knowledge Café

Protocols *really provide a structure for teacher conversations that give everyone a chance to participate and equalize the "air time" each member of the group gets. The protocols focus teachers' attention on certain dilemmas and provide an opportunity to provide important feedback through something called "critical friendship."*

—Terry Campanella, Broward County Public Schools Coach

Organizational tools like open-space technology *and the* knowledge café *are processes used at our school for professional development. Teachers work together to learn more about ideas or topics of interest. It is not about having great meetings nor is it another tool in a facilitators' toolbox, although both are doubtlessly true. What I connect to is the ongoing-learning experience of learning intentionally in a self-organizing world.*

—Donnan Stoicovy, Park Forest Elementary Principal

Terry and Donnan recognize that protocols, open-space technology (OST), and other conversation tools like the knowledge café are powerful vehicles for generating professional knowledge within the schools' walls. Indeed, these professional development tools can intentionally shape the back-porch conversations that lead to teacher learning. Although the origins of these tools are quite different, these tools might be considered "kissing cousins" as they are closely akin to one another in their ability to generate collaborative discussion and reflection between professionals.

DEFINITION: CONVERSATION TOOLS

In the last decade, conversation tools have emerged from within both the education and the organizational literature as professional development tools that offer structured conversation steps to explore a chosen topic and accomplish a particular learning-related purpose.

Protocols

Protocols have emerged from the education literature and are tools that educators often use to enable and strengthen communication between colleagues focused on important dilemmas of practice.

Joseph McDonald and his colleagues (McDonald, Mohr, Dichter, & McDonald, 2003) explain the importance of using protocols:

> In diplomacy, protocol governs who greets whom first when the President and Prime Minister meet, and other such matters. In technology, protocols enable machines to "talk" with one another by precisely defining the language they use. In science and medicine, protocols are regimens that ensure faithful replication of an experiment or treatment; they tell the scientist or doctor to do this first, then that, and so on. And in social science, they are the scripted questions that an interviewer covers, or the template for an observation.
>
> But in the professional education of educators, one could argue that elaborate etiquette, communication precision, faithful replication, and scripts would prove counterproductive here. Don't we best learn from each other by just talking with each other? No, we claim. Among educators especially, just talking may not be enough. The kind of talking needed to educate ourselves cannot rise spontaneously and unaided from just talking. It needs to be carefully planned and scaffolded. (McDonald et al., 2003, p. 4)

Like McDonald and his colleagues, our work with protocols has made clear the importance of intentionally planned and scaffolded conversations by and for teachers in schools. We learned this by observing the National School Reform Faculty's (NSRF) protocol use.

The NSRF is an organization committed to developing collegial relationships, encouraging reflective practice, and rethinking leadership in restructuring schools. Their work with protocols reflects their serious commitment to involve educators in professional conversations targeted at enhancing student learning. The NSRF protocols, created by educators for educators, help teachers deeply explore four key sources of teacher learning: (1) learning from work, (2) learning from dilemmas, (3) learning from texts, and (4) learning from school and classroom visits (see www.nsrfharmony.org/protocols.html). The teachers select different protocols for use by matching the nature of the professional learning sought with the protocol's purpose.

Open-Space Technology and Knowledge Cafés

In contrast to protocols, open-space technology (OST) and knowledge cafés emerged from the organizational literature. OST is a tool used to help facilitate learning-community meetings by using an open-ended format. It relies on group members bringing their dilemmas and solutions to the meeting to facilitate collaboration. The term *technology* in this case refers to the open nature of the process or method used rather than the use of digital technology.

OST provides educators with additional conversation tools that can help strengthen job-embedded professional learning. It is described as follows.

> Open Space Technology was created in the mid-1980s by organizational consultant Harrison Owen when he discovered that people attending his conferences loved the coffee breaks better than the formal presentations and plenary sessions. . . .
>
> Open Space conferences have no keynote speakers, no preannounced schedules of workshops, no panel discussions, and no organizational booths. (Co-Intelligence Institute, 2003–2008, para 1–2)

As indicated, OST is a conversation tool that allows the group to determine an agenda and create their own meeting or conference based on their immediate needs and interests. Almost before they realize it, educators become each other's teachers and leaders.

The knowledge café is also drawn from the organizational literature. When applied to work in schools, the knowledge café gathers teachers together to provide an open and creative marketplace of ideas to be shared related to a topic of mutual interest. The structured, small-group conversations surface a group's collective knowledge, as participants in the process share ideas and insights and gain a deeper understanding of the subject and the issues involved.

Each of these conversation tools—protocols, open-space technology, and knowledge cafés—are designed to provide important structure to the conversations that educators have in schools, so that conversation is focused and deliberate, not happenstance. Indeed, these tools are important in helping teachers process as well as create knowledge *for* and *of* practice.

ILLUSTRATION: CONVERSATION TOOLS

Protocols

Let's begin by visiting with a group of elementary teachers in south Florida who were collectively struggling with how to create inclusive middle schools while at the same time surviving the pressures associated with high-stakes testing and accountability. Given that both the problem of high-stakes testing and inclusion were not going to go away, the group's facilitator, Terry Campenella, selected a National School Reform Faculty (NSRF) protocol designed to help educators collaboratively "learn from texts."

Terry began by sharing the charge for the day: "We need to develop a shared understanding of inclusion as well as ways in which our individual and collective beliefs and assumptions may differ within our school."

Given that the goal was to understand the concept of inclusion more deeply, the group read a short article written by Nancy Waldron and James McLeskey (1998) titled, "The Effects of Inclusive School Programs on Students With Mild and Severe Learning Disabilities." Like the book study, the goal of the reading was to create knowledge for practice about inclusion of students with disabilities in general-education classrooms.

As group members read the article on inclusion, they highlighted and wrote notes in the margin to answer the following four questions (the protocol used to structure this text discussion, "The four 'A's'" can be found at www.nsrfharmony.org/protocol/doc/4_a_text.pdf):

1. What *assumptions* does the author of the text hold?

2. What do you *agree* with in the text?

3. What do you want to *argue* with in the text?

4. What parts of the text do you want to *aspire* to?

Once each person had a chance to read the article and jot down their thoughts related to the four As, the group began a series of rounds talking about the text in light of each of the As, beginning with assumptions and taking the other three one at a time. This allowed the teachers to respond to the article's presentation of inclusion. During the discussion, teachers had opportunities to honestly "hear" and understand their colleagues' perspectives, which was a critical first step to professional learning and collaboration.

At the end of all four rounds, Terry led a general discussion focused on the question, "What does this mean for our work with students?" The group debriefed the activity by identifying how they might improve the discussion in the future as well as what their next steps would be toward understanding the nuances of creating inclusive schools.

Although the "Four 'A's'" protocol helped educators explore existing knowledge for practice by examining text, other protocols explore different kinds of professional knowledge construction. For example, sometimes educators experience dilemmas of practice, and NSRF also offers protocols that focus on "learning from dilemmas." Let's examine another example of protocol use focused on a different group of teachers and the dilemma of one of the group's members, Cheryl.

Cheryl asked if she could share a dilemma of practice during her grade-level team meeting. She was interested in a conversation related to some felt difficulties she was having in regards to improving her writing instruction. She posed the question, "How do I improve the narrative writing of my students?"

She asked her grade-level team to use the "The Collaborative Assessment Conference," another protocol created by the National School Reform Faculty, to shape the conversation they engaged in at their meeting. She brought to the conversation examples of a student's writing as data for the group to review.

Following the first step of this protocol, Cheryl selected one student from her class to focus on, and passed out copies of her selected student's writing to members of her grade-level team. She said nothing about the work, the context in which it was created, or the student. The group members read the work in silence, making brief notes about aspects that were particularly striking to them.

In Step 2 of the protocol, titled "Describing the Work," the facilitator asked "What do you see?" Group members provided answers without making judgments about the quality of the work. If a judgment emerged, the facilitator asked for the evidence on which the judgment was based.

In Step 3, called "Asking Questions About the Work," the facilitator asked the group, "What questions does this work raise for you?" Group members stated questions they had about the work, the child, the assignment, and the circumstances under which the work was created.

In Step 4, titled "Speculating," the facilitator asked the group, "What do you think the child is working on?" Group members made suggestions about the problems or issues that the student might have been focused on in carrying out the assignment. During Steps 3, 4, and 5, Cheryl listened carefully and took notes, but was not allowed to respond.

In Step 5, the facilitator invited Cheryl to speak about her perspective on the student's work, describing what she saw in it, responding to one or more of the questions raised, and adding any other information she thought was important for the group to know. Cheryl also commented on the surprising and unexpected things that she heard during the describing, questioning, and speculating steps of the protocol. Included in her comments was her emerging appreciation for more specifically developed rubrics as well as ideas for leading focused individual-writing conferences during the school day.

In the final steps of the protocol, the facilitator invited everyone to share new thoughts they had about their own writing instruction, writing in general, or ways to support this particular child in the future. The protocol discussion ended with the group reflecting on the "Collaborative Assessment Conference" protocol and thanking Cheryl, the presenting teacher, for sharing her student's work and her teaching dilemma.

Open-Space Technology

Just as the protocols created by the NSRF provide tools to generate professional learning through conversation, so does open-space technology (OST). At one of the schools we work with, the staff uses OST during a faculty meeting to help explore the school's current technology integration.

As faculty entered the room for their monthly meeting at Park Forest Elementary School, they noticed one wall covered with blank chart paper. They knew their principal, Donnan, had set the room up in this fashion to have an OST meeting. The blank chart paper, referred to as a "news wall," would be used for the faculty members to develop an agenda for their meeting as well as to capture the nature of the discussions they would have in smaller groups focused on the topic of the meeting—integrating technology into instruction.

The principal, Donnan, began, "The dilemma we are investigating today is how to better utilize technology with our students, and I would like any of you who have topics related to this question—that you would like to facilitate a discussion about—please come up to our news wall and jot them down." Immediately, teachers began walking up to the blank white chart paper wall at the front of the room and writing topics for discussions they wished to facilitate. For example, Barbara, a third-grade teacher wrote, "Having Laptop Literature Discussions During Reading Time." Fourth-grade teacher, Sheila, followed with "Integrating Technology Into Our Communications With Parents."

A total of five teachers named specific technology issues and questions that they wanted to explore during today's time together. In addition to the topics already named, other topics included removing barriers to and providing facilitators with technology integration, technology integration in math and science, and technology use in student portfolio work.

These five teachers became the "conveners" of the discussions around their issues. On the news wall, they noted the location of another classroom in the building where they could lead a discussion with others on their topic. The remaining teachers were asked to visit the agenda wall and sign up for the session they wanted to attend.

The session discussions began and note takers were quickly identified to capture each group's conversation. The conversations explored these multiple technology topics. By the end of the discussions, the recorders collapsed the conversations into key points, used bullets to highlight actionable ideas generated, and returned to the faculty room to post these summaries on the news wall for others to review.

When everyone was settled back in the faculty room, each group took a turn to highlight the key areas and the action plans that had been discussed in their small groups. As group members shared their action plans, they assigned tasks in the action plan to people who could move the idea forward toward implementation. This portion of the OST meeting created a sense of closure by reviewing the contents from the news wall as all faculty members shared their comments, insights, and commitments to the actions outlined.

Knowledge Cafés

Similar to an OST meeting, knowledge cafés can be utilized to shape the conversation that occurs between faculty members at a school. As a final illustration of a conversation tool that can facilitate professional learning, let's watch a knowledge café in action within a school that is interested in infusing problem-based learning across their curriculum.

Problem-based learning (PBL) is a student-centered instructional strategy in which students collaboratively solve problems and reflect on their experiences. Typically, PBL requires teachers to redefine teaching so that student learning is driven by complex, open-ended problems that students work collaboratively to solve with the scaffolding and facilitation of the teacher.

The knowledge café begins as the principal welcomes her faculty to their October faculty meeting and shares,

> Today we will use the knowledge café to generate a conversation that will uncover and share our knowledge related to implementing problem-based learning. There is important knowledge within our faculty built upon experiences you have had already with PBL as an instructional approach. We will spend today exploring that existing knowledge in a way that will push our work forward.

The principal goes on to explain that the knowledge café will focus on the following five issues that collectively explore the concept of how, together, they can strengthen their PBL work. The issues are introduced by the following questions:

1. How do I safeguard the integrity of the process?
2. What part do hands-on instructional materials and kits play in PBL?
3. What can we do to facilitate cross-curriculum PBL efforts?
4. What tools have proven effective in assessing PBL?
5. How do we effectively integrate technology into PBL so that it adds value to the process?

After introducing these issues, the principal broke the faculty into five groups, each consisting of five to eight educators. These small groups met and discussed one of the issues for about twenty minutes. Although not led by a facilitator, each table selected a recorder who captured the ideas generated in their conversation on a large piece of chart paper.

After twenty minutes, all but one of the participants from each group moved to another table to discuss a different question. The group member that remained at the table shared the contents of the last conversation held at the table with the new group. This allowed the new group to recognize and build on the knowledge already created in the prior discussion. This process continued through five rounds of small-group discussion.

At the conclusion of the knowledge café, the groups posted their ideas around the room and the participants moved around, reviewing the work posted. At the end of the meeting, the faculty reflected on their learning by sharing thoughts, insights, and ideas on the topic that emerged. A copy of the ideas were then typed up and distributed to the faculty. At a next meeting, the group might create individual and collective action steps. According to David Gurteen, a senior consultant of knowledge management as group processing, the most important rule is that the café is conducted so that most of the time is spent in conversation!

WHAT HAVE WE LEARNED?

Table 6.1 illustrates how these conversation tools help those engaged in planning job-embedded professional learning attend to the knowledge building blocks. In reviewing Table 6.1, we see that the building blocks addressed through conversation tools are "bookends" for both source of knowledge and learning needs. For those interested in creating job-embedded professional learning, these conversation tools are essential to assuring that important building blocks are not skipped or underestimated. Although these tools share the purpose of strengthening teacher knowledge through conversation, the tools need to be carefully matched with the specific kind of knowledge that needs to be created.

Table 6.1 Protocols, Open-Space Technology, and Knowledge Cafés: Building Blocks for Powerful Professional Learning

Building-Block Type	Building Blocks						Theorists
Learning Needs	Understanding of research-based practice	View model	Practice time	Feedback and Coaching	Collaborative conversation and reflection		Borko (2004); Desimone (2009); Joyce and Showers (1983)
Orientation	Outside orientation			Inside orientation			Marzano, Pickering, and Pollock (2001); Cochran-Smith and Lytle (1999, 2001, 2009)
Type of Knowledge	Pedagogical knowledge	Curriculum knowledge	Student knowledge	Content knowledge	Context knowledge	Pedagogical content knowledge	Grossman (1990); Magnusson, Krajcik, and Borko (1999); Shulman (1987a, 1987b)
Source of Knowledge	Knowledge for practice		Knowledge in practice		Knowledge of practice		Cochran-Smith and Lytle (1999, 2001, 2009)

When choosing conversation tools as a part of your professional-development toolbox, you are recognizing that important knowledge is available inside your school, and you can strengthen teaching, learning, and relationships by exploring this knowledge together. As you witnessed in these illustrations, teachers were able to collaboratively learn about inclusive school reform, improve writing pedagogy, strengthen a school's efforts related to technology integration, and shape one another's knowledge related to problem-based learning. Conversations, when well structured and focused on important goals, contribute to professional learning that is powerful enough to change practice. In returning to McDonald and colleagues' (2003) insights presented at the beginning of this chapter, we must all recognize that structured conversations are critical to the success of learning on our metaphorical back porch.

SOME THINGS TO THINK ABOUT

- *What is the degree of comfort that exists with these tools at your school?*

Creating a level of readiness to use conversation tools at your school will require a shift away from teachers expecting external authorities to deliver knowledge toward teachers expecting themselves to engage in active listening and sharing that can shape the professional knowledge within their schools. Not only will this require a commitment from teachers, but there will be an equally important need for commitment toward job-embedded learning from the building leadership. Additionally, although protocols, open-space technology, and knowledge cafés are tools for teachers to collaboratively shape their own professional learning, these tools will require teachers to understand that the kind of conversation needed to strengthen teaching and learning will not rise spontaneously and unaided from the traditional talk of schools. The conversations need to be carefully planned, structured, and scaffolded in order for deep professional learning to occur.

- *How ready is your school's culture to implement the tool?*

A school's culture can make or break the successful use of conversation tools to influence teacher learning. Some key beliefs that should be alive and well in your school are (1) the importance of identifying and raising questions, (2) the power of collaboration, (3) an affinity toward open conversation and listening to others, (4) a willingness to make learning and problems public, and (5) a culture that encourages as well as facilitates teachers' efforts to make changes in their teaching practices.

- *How would you carve out time to use these tools in your building?*

Although time always seems to be a challenge, those interested in using conversation tools can find time within the school day to create these back-porch conversations. By involving teachers in rethinking the way existing time is used, teachers can identify when conversations can be held that focus on learning rather than logistics and management tasks. Some examples are restructured team meetings, faculty meetings, and professional development days.

- *What resources would you need to successfully use these tools?*

Successful use of conversation tools relies on you, as a leader of job-embedded learning in your school, having sophisticated knowledge of conversation tools and how to match the protocols, open-space technology, and knowledge café to specific teacher learning needs in a timely manner. Once you have gained this knowledge, it will be critical that you build capacity for selecting conversation tools in others.

- *What type of data might you collect while using these tools?*

As you integrate the use of conversation tools into the professional learning at your school, it is important to identify the kinds of data you can collect to guide your next professional development efforts as well as determine if these conversations are leading to student and teacher learning. In reflecting on the illustrations presented in this chapter, you might collect the following data: writing samples, writing test scores, lesson plans that indicate technology use, artifacts that demonstrate progress toward standards implementation, as well as changes in teachers' beliefs and knowledge of inclusion.

ADDITIONAL RESOURCES

Web Sites

Annenberg Institute for School Reform. http://www.lasw.org.

Gurteen's Knowledge Café. http://www.gurteen.com/gurteen/gurteen.nsf/id/kcafe.

I&DEA, Knowledge Café. http://www.idea.gov.uk/idk/core/page.do?pageId=8155478.

Looking at Student Work. http://www.lasw.org/methods.html.

NSRF Protocols. http://www.nsrfharmony.org.

Open Space World. http://www.openspaceworld.org/cgi/wiki.cgi?AboutOpen Space.

Publications

McDonald, J. P., Mohr, N., Dichter, A., & McDonald, E. C. (2003). *The power of protocols: An educator's guide to better practice.* New York: Teachers College Press.

Owen, H. (1997). *Open space technology: A user's guide.* San Francisco: Berrett-Koehler.

7

Lesson Study

Lesson study *is an approach to professional development in which groups of teachers engage in systematic study of their practice. It is a job-embedded, teacher-driven approach to improving instructional practice. While it uses a lesson as its focus, the significance of lesson study is the ongoing process of researching and studying practice rather than the production of a single lesson. Lesson study has the potential to improve teachers' knowledge of content, knowledge of curriculum, knowledge of pedagogy, and knowledge of students. Lesson study is a way of creating a culture of commitment to continued professional growth. It provides a collaborative forum in which teachers can meaningfully connect theory to practice.*

—Johnna Boylard, Mathematics Professor, Coach,
and Professional Development School Liaison

Johnna's thoughts acknowledge the power that lesson study has as a collaborative, job-embedded, professional development tool that brings together teachers interested in strengthening the impact of their instruction. The tool creates an inquiry orientation to lesson development as well as produces a lesson that can be shared with others. Indeed, we have explored a tool earlier in this text that shares many similarities with lesson study, coteaching. However, lesson study differs from coteaching in that the lesson study team is a group of teachers rather than a dyad, and the group works through multiple iterations of a single lesson to perfect the lesson's ability to impact student learning.

In Chapter 7, we explore lesson study as a tool that provides job-embedded learning as a group of teachers work side by side to plan, teach, observe, and study the outcomes of particular instructional episodes. Lesson study is a professional development tool that has the power to cultivate knowledge *for*, *in*, and *of* practice. To help you understand the nuances of this tool, we will define lesson study and then provide an illustration of how a school might use this tool to strengthen teaching practice.

DEFINITION: LESSON STUDY

Lesson study is a professional development strategy that allows teachers to systematically and collaboratively examine and improve their teaching practice. Teachers create study lessons together by planning, teaching, observing, critiquing, and revising the lessons as a group. This spiraling process is driven by an overarching goal and a research question shaped by the group. The end result is not only a better-developed lesson; typically, teachers also come away with a stronger understanding of the content, enhanced observation skills, stronger collegial networks, and a tighter connection between daily practice and long-term goals (Lewis, Perry, & Hurd, 2004). The lesson study typically culminates with a report that summarizes what the study taught them.

ILLUSTRATION: LESSON STUDY

Schools that possess a collaborative culture are the best contexts for implementing lesson study. Let's visit with the teachers at Harper Middle School to understand how they have embedded lesson study into their school's professional learning culture.

One of the school's mathematics teachers, Jessica Gold, had recently attended a summer workshop where she was introduced to lesson study. Although she was one of the least-experienced teachers on her team, with only four years of experience, she was a true teacher leader and decided that she would encourage her colleagues to implement this professional development tool as a part of their regular team-planning activities. Although time was precious, with some convincing her team decided that they would embrace the idea, carve lesson study time out of their shared-planning time one day each week, and set out together to improve their math instruction.

The group began by framing the goal of their research lesson, which was "Students will develop an interest in understanding how to apply mathematical discourse to real-world situations." The teachers realized that many times middle school students become apathetic to their learning and that infusing problem-based, applied learning might enhance engagement and ultimately facilitate stronger mathematical discourse that demonstrated mathematical understanding in applied contexts. This was a great research problem to guide their lesson study because the math team knew they would need each other's support to begin shifting their approach away from the textbook to teaching more applied middle school mathematics that facilitated applied mathematical conversations among students.

Their group began by discussing what good evidence would be for assessing their progress toward creating flexibility in mathematical language and application. Because they were interested in mathematical language, they knew they should focus on what the students were doing, saying, and showing each other. Specifically, in the first round of the math lesson study, they wanted students to engage in mathematical discourse, and they wanted to hear the students' flexibility in movement between math languages like fraction language, decimal language, percent, or money language. Within this applied lesson, the middle school math team hoped to hear all of their students using the language interchangeably as they demonstrated the math concept.

Once they had determined their goal and the data that they would collect, the group began collaborative lesson planning. Together, they were able to develop a lesson they believed would generate student dialogue around an applied problem that demonstrated flexibility in movement between mathematical languages.

The process was not easy for them at first. The lesson study required them to begin by planning a single lesson together that would be differentiated across grade levels as well as courses in both algebra and geometry. The teachers were not accustomed to planning and teaching a shared lesson, and many of the group members had to let go of their independent approach to instructional planning. However, with time and patience during the next two weeks, the teachers collaboratively crafted a problem-based math lesson that, along the way, deepened their own understanding of the content and also the application of the mathematics content to an applied problem that would enhance student ability to flexibly apply mathematical language and concepts.

Up to this point, the teachers had been able to reallocate existing time they had in their planning period to collaboratively develop the lesson. However, the observation period would be problematic in that four members of the lesson study group, all math teachers, would need coverage for the same period. They also knew that this would happen four times. With this in mind, Jessica and her team met with the principal to discuss the dilemma of coverage. By sharing the process and the potential gains that would emerge as a result of the lesson study, the principal helped them creatively plan coverage for their classrooms. Although they explored a variety of options to cover the classrooms using other school faculty, the principal decided that he would use school-based professional development funds to provide four substitutes for the afternoon of the observed lesson. That way, the group would have time to not only observe the lesson but also debrief immediately during Jessica's planning period and after school.

Given their goals and the time now allotted by the principal, the group needed to identify the specifics of their observation plan. After some discussion, the lesson study group members believed the most important data would be to listen to and record student conversations. To capture both types of data, three of the teachers observed and recorded student language verbatim, and the fourth charted time, to document persistence. For each lesson in their four-lesson sequence, the group was trying to increase this language and increase student persistence to solve an applied problem.

Jessica taught the lesson first to her students as the research team observed. They made many notes by anecdotally recording the students' conversations. Sometimes, they even asked the children clarifying questions to capture what the students were really thinking as they worked in their groups.

Once the lesson was completed, the teachers gathered in the conference room for a debriefing. At this time, they reviewed all the data, discussed the implications and what they were learning, and then made revisions as a result of reflecting on the process. This information helped them identify their concerns for the next lesson. One of the teachers noted,

> I really noticed that there was a lot of enthusiasm for the lesson in the beginning; but eventually, many of the students had questions, and some became less persistent in solving the problem over time. There was also a subset of students who seemed to let the others take charge. I would like to take a look at their written work more closely to see if they understood the mathematics concepts. Perhaps, a lack of understanding is why some students' persistence began to fade.

Although a large number of the students were highly engaged and asking high-level questions, the observers weren't sure that the less-involved students were "getting it." The group engaged in a long discussion as to whether the problem-based task was relevant to the students and how they could better prepare them for applying the content.

At the end of that conversation, the team celebrated their successes, and the group revised several portions of the lesson. Some of the adjustments were logistical, others were instructional, but the teachers' conversation about the content seemed to create a real shift in their thinking about why middle school students sometimes don't "get it" and how to draw them into a mathematics way of thinking. At the conclusion of the meeting, Sam volunteered to teach the revised lesson the following week. The group was excited to observe what happened when the adjusted lesson was taught. Given that the lesson study repeated four times, the lesson study group members aimed for lesson improvement related to the research question each time.

WHAT HAVE WE LEARNED?

Lesson study as a professional development tool helps teachers collaboratively develop new professional knowledge by systematically studying a particular lesson. As teachers plan together, observe, and debrief, they typically identify and pinpoint shifts in their thinking about the instruction, the curriculum, the context, the content, and their students. Together, they create shared knowledge that integrates the building blocks of professional learning (see Table 7.1). Additionally, the lesson study also creates private moments for reflection after the conversations have ended. Together, this learning influences the next round of teaching. As the group's knowledge strengthens so does their instruction. In sum, lesson study is about struggling to understand the teaching and learning process through a collaborative and inquiry-driven approach. The process is time intensive, but as indicated in Table 7.1, lesson study has the power to develop each of our knowledge building blocks.

SOME THINGS TO THINK ABOUT

- *What is the degree of comfort that exists with this tool at your school?*

Since lesson study is relatively new and not a regularly visible professional development tool that most educators have witnessed, the odds are that little comfort exists in your school related to both how to facilitate the use of the tool and how to participate in the study group itself. Thus, the facilitator would benefit by reading about lesson study, watching videos of lesson study in action, piloting the activity, as well as sharing these materials with the lesson study group members before beginning the cycle.

- *How ready is your school's culture to implement the tool?*

Not only will lesson study require a collaborative culture but it will also require school leadership that values collaborative learning. Given that resources will be needed to relieve teachers from instructional duties during the day for lesson observation, those involved in dispersing resources must see the tool as worth the time. There must be a perceived bang for the buck. Additionally, teachers who successfully use lesson study feel comfortable sharing their classroom as well as their instructional planning with others. This often requires a shift in the way teachers perceive their instructional responsibilities.

Table 7.1 Lesson Study: Building Blocks for Powerful Professional Learning

Building-Block Type	Building Blocks						Theorists
Learning Needs	Understanding of research-based practice		View model	Practice time	Feedback and Coaching	Collaborative conversation and reflection	Borko (2004); Desimone (2009); Joyce and Showers (1983)
Orientation	Outside orientation			Inside orientation			Marzano, Pickering, and Pollock (2001); Cochran-Smith and Lytle (1999, 2001, 2009)
Type of Knowledge	Pedagogical knowledge	Curriculum knowledge	Student knowledge	Content knowledge	Context knowledge	Pedagogical content knowledge	Grossman (1990); Magnusson, Krajcik, and Borko (1999); Shulman (1987a, 1987b)
Source of Knowledge	Knowledge for practice			Knowledge in practice	Knowledge of practice		Cochran-Smith and Lytle (1999, 2001, 2009)

- *How would you carve out time to use this tool in your building?*

As you could see in this illustration, the teachers were instrumental in securing the necessary time for their lesson study. They initiated a meeting with the school leadership to request time and figure out how they would cover classes so teachers could observe the lesson being taught. As the teachers were able to share the power of lesson study as related to student learning, the principal's response was to provide a set of substitutes to support the teachers' lesson study activity. In this case, he used Title II funds to support the lesson study activities.

- *What resources would you need to successfully use this tool?*

Lesson study is a sophisticated process that will require facilitator and teacher knowledge of the process. Human resources are, once again, the most important elements needed for lesson study. That said, the composition of the lesson study group is important. You will want to be sure that there are group participants with differentiated expertise in as many of the knowledge types as possible: pedagogical, curricular, student, content, and context. By having expertise present across these areas, the group is more likely to construct a lesson that blends these knowledge types in a way that strengthens student learning.

- *What type of data might you collect while using this tool?*

Data is at the heart of any lesson study. As teachers embrace an inquiry orientation to their professional development, they rely on data that result from the lesson to engage in feedback as well as collaborative conversation and reflection. The data is the student work as well as the anecdotal observations collected by the study team. Over time, curriculum-based assessments can also be collected to measure student learning. Although data collection should focus on student-level data, intermediate outcomes in the form of enhanced teacher professional knowledge can also be collected after each study cycle.

ADDITIONAL RESOURCES

Web Sites

Lesson Study Group at Mills College. http://www.lessonresearch.net.
Lesson Study Research Group. http://www.tc.columbia.edu/lessonstudy/index.html.

Publications

Lewis, C., Perry, R., & Hurd, J. (2004). A deeper look at lesson study. *Educational Leadership, 61*(5), 18.
Stepanek, J., Appel, G., Leong, M., Mangan, M. T., & Mitchell, M. (2007). *Leading lesson study: A practical guide for teachers and facilitators*. Thousand Oaks, CA: Corwin.

8

Teacher Inquiry/ Action Research

Very simply put, inquiry *is a way for me to continue growing as a teacher. Before I became involved in* action research, *I'd gotten to the point where I'd go to an inservice and shut off my brain. Most of the teachers I know have been at the same place. If you have been around at all, you know that most inservices are the same cheese—just repackaged. Inquiry lets me choose my own growth and gives me tools to validate or jettison my ideas.*

—John Kreinbihl, Anderson Elementary School Teacher

Action research *is a superpower. Whether a teacher is just starting out or is a 30-year veteran, action research provides teachers with opportunities to explore changes in their practice as well as a voice to change the world of teaching.*

—Kevin Berry, Alachua Elementary School Teacher

John and Kevin make an excellent case for why you should consider introducing or integrating teacher inquiry, also known as action research, into your school's job-embedded, professional development efforts. These educators recognize the power of action research in transforming teaching practice. Whether completed individually or collaboratively, action research allows a teacher to raise questions about his or her teaching and come up with solutions for improving it. Like lesson study, action research has the power to cultivate knowledge *for, in,* and *of* practice. In Chapter 8, we define action research and then provide an illustration of how a school might utilize action research to strengthen teaching practice.

DEFINITION: TEACHER INQUIRY/ACTION RESEARCH

Teacher inquiry, also referred to as action research, teacher research, or practitioner inquiry, is defined as systematic, intentional study by teachers of their own classroom practice (Cochran-Smith & Lytle, 1993). In using this tool, educators seek out change and reflect on their practice by posing questions or "wonderings," collecting data to gain insights into their wonderings, analyzing the data along with reading relevant literature, making changes in practice based on new understandings developed during inquiry, and sharing findings with others (Dana & Yendol-Hoppey, 2009). This tool has demonstrated over and over again that it is powerful enough to change both teaching practice and student learning.

ILLUSTRATION: TEACHER INQUIRY/ACTION RESEARCH

To illustrate this process, we turn to teacher researcher Debbi Hubbell. Debbi teaches fourth grade in a rural elementary school located in north Florida. Intrigued when her principal offered the opportunity to engage in teacher research as a part of staff development at her building, Debbi decided to look closely at one of her teaching passions: reading. Debbi knew that one of the best predictors of performance on Florida's yearly standardized test, the FCAT (Florida Comprehensive Assessment Test), was reading fluency and that research has shown a direct correlation between fluency and comprehension. She wanted to help her students become more successful in reading and perform better on the FCAT.

Worried about seven students she felt were at risk and less fluent than others in her class, she decided to introduce the rereading of fractured fairy tale plays to these learners to see if this activity might increase reading fluency. As is common for learners at risk, these seven students had been engaged almost exclusively in more traditional skill-and-drill literacy activities.

To gain insights into her research question—"What is the relationship between my fourth-graders' fluency development and the reading of fractured fairy tale plays?"—Debbi collected three forms of data. First, Debbi administered Dynamic Indicators of Basic Early Literacy Skills (DIBELS) at different times throughout her research. DIBELS are a set of standardized, individually administered measures of early literacy development. They are designed to be short (one minute) fluency measures used to regularly monitor the development of prereading and early reading skills. In addition, Debbi took anecdotal notes each time she utilized fractured fairy tale plays with these fourth-grade students, documenting their reactions, engagement, and Debbi's assessment of their fluency development with each rereading of a play. Finally, Debbi relied on student work or artifacts as a third data source. At the end of the fractured fairy tale series, Debbi asked her students to write "Dear Mrs. Hubbell" letters, telling her about their perceptions and experiences with the fractured fairy tale unit of study.

Debbi analyzed her data by charting student DIBELS scores over time as well as through organizing and reading through her anecdotal notes and student-produced artifacts. Based on her data, Debbi was able to make three statements about what she learned as a result of her research. First, all students' DIBELS scores improved over time. Second, the reading of fractured fairy tale plays generated enthusiasm for school and learning. A student who had said he hated school and was failing actually said later he enjoyed reading fractured fairy tales and producing them as a play. This student improved at least by a grade or more in *each* subject. Third, positive social interactions occurred between students who previously had difficulty communicating in a positive way. Students enjoyed helping each other when someone made a mistake in word recognition, stress, pitch, or phrasing, and tolerance as well as admiration replaced existing adversarial student-to-student relationships.

As her inquiry progressed and Debbi's data indicated the academic, social, and emotional value of teaching with fractured fairy tales, Debbi began implementing fractured fairy tale plays with her entire class, in addition to the seven learners who were the focus of her inquiry.

At the close of the school year, Debbi shared what she had learned during her inquiry into the relationship between the reading of fractured fairy tale plays and the fluency development of struggling fourth-grade readers at a local action-research conference, receiving solid feedback on her inquiry from other teachers (Hubbell, 2005). Next, Debbie shared her research at a faculty meeting in her school. Her inquiry served as the impetus for her school to develop schoolwide fluency objectives and engage in dialogue to assess existing reading practices in her school and district.

In reflection, Debbie Hubbell (as cited in Dana & Yendol-Hoppey, 2009) sheds light on how inquiry naturally has found space in her professional life:

> Teacher inquiry is not something I do; it is more a part of the way I think. Inquiry involves exciting and meaningful discussions with colleagues about the passions we embrace in our profession. It has become the gratifying response to formalizing the questions that

enter my mind as I teach. It is a learning process that keeps me passionate about teaching. (p. 6)

WHAT HAVE WE LEARNED?

Teacher inquiry, as a professional development tool, helps teachers create new professional knowledge through systematic study. Educators can use these tools to encourage all types of knowledge construction—pedagogical, curricular, content, context, or student knowledge—as they reflect on either what they have observed or what they have taught. The tool brings to light both an external and internal orientation to knowledge as practitioners bring to the forefront both a knowledge of research in the area of inquiry as well as create new professional knowledge related to implementing changes in their classrooms. Table 8.1 shows that each of the knowledge building blocks can be accomplished using teacher inquiry as long as the cycle of posing questions (or wonderings), collecting data to gain insights into wonderings, analyzing data along with reading relevant literature, making changes in practice based on new understandings developed during inquiry, and sharing findings with others is completed.

SOME THINGS TO THINK ABOUT

• *What is the degree of comfort that exists with this tool at your school?*

Although teacher inquiry has been around for many years, schools have not typically integrated the inquiry process into their school-based, professional development efforts. In some contexts, the process of action research may initially seem too time intensive. However, by rethinking teacher inquiry as a naturally occurring activity that teachers engage in as a part of their teaching, the work truly becomes job embedded. Before expecting teachers to engage in teacher research, it will be helpful to spend time introducing the process and providing the necessary coaching as teachers move their way through the process. Comfort with teacher inquiry will occur as educators are provided the necessary knowledge or skills to systematically plan or carry out a study independently.

• *How ready is your school's culture to implement the tool?*

As with many of the tools explored in this book, the success of integrating teacher inquiry into the fabric of your school will rest on the nature of your school as an organization. If your school has been successful in cultivating a professional disposition toward learning and can provide the necessary supports for teachers to be successful, then the culture is ripe for

Table 8.1   Teacher Inquiry: Building Blocks for Powerful Professional Learning

Building-Block Type	Building Blocks						Theorists
Learning Needs	Understanding of research-based practice		View model	Practice time	Feedback and Coaching	Collaborative conversation and reflection	Borko (2004); Desimone (2009); Joyce and Showers (1983)
Orientation	Outside orientation		Inside orientation				Marzano, Pickering, and Pollock (2001); Cochran-Smith and Lytle (1999, 2001, 2009)
Type of Knowledge	Pedagogical knowledge	Curriculum knowledge	Student knowledge	Content knowledge	Context knowledge	Pedagogical content knowledge	Grossman (1990); Magnusson, Krajcik, and Borko (1999); Shulman (1987a, 1987b)
Source of Knowledge	Knowledge for practice		Knowledge in practice		Knowledge of practice		Cochran-Smith and Lytle (1999, 2001, 2009)

introducing this tool. If your school is in the process of cultivating a learning community, we suggest piloting teacher research with a group of teachers and then expanding that group overtime.

- *How would you carve out time to use this tool in your building?*

When it comes to job-embedded learning tools such as teacher inquiry, time is really less of a factor. We need to think of teacher inquiry as a part of rather than apart from or something in addition to what successful teachers do. When teacher inquiry is conceived of in this way, identifying problems of practice, learning from the research base, testing out solutions, collecting naturally occurring data, and making sense of the data to inform practice should be easily integrated into an educator's work day. Any time that is required outside of the school day to support teacher inquiry can be culled using the ideas presented in Chapter 3.

- *What resources would you need to successfully use this tool?*

Resources are available to make this kind of professional development possible. For example, in order to make teacher inquiry a part of a teacher's professional life, we must be prepared to build the structures that support job-embedded teacher learning. Gail Ritchie and the teachers with whom she works with in Fairfax County Schools have figured this out. Let's eavesdrop on Gail's reflections on the successes that they have made to embed teacher research into the profession:

> For at least 15 years, maybe longer, the district has funded "release time" for teachers who are members of site-based (school-based) teacher-research groups. Through this school year, the district has paid for three full days (which most people take as six half days) for each teacher researcher. This allows the researchers to meet together monthly, on school time, with substitute teachers (who are paid for by the district) covering their classes.

When district and school leadership see value in a professional development tool, they are more likely to provide the necessary resources.

- *What type of data might you collect while using this tool?*

It is actually fairly easy to think about data when engaged in teacher inquiry, as data collection is a necessary and natural part of the inquiry cycle. Data for most action-research efforts include student work, anecdotal or field notes, curriculum-based assessments, progress monitoring, and lesson plans. As you can see, this data is naturally occurring in classrooms and, as a result, is easy to capture as long as you have a systematic plan.

Action research can also include other types of data that may not be as naturally occurring in the classroom, such as interviews and surveys.

ADDITIONAL RESOURCES

Web Sites

George Mason Teacher Research. http://gse.gmu.edu/research/tr.
National Writing Project Teacher Inquiry Communities. http://www.nwp.org/cs/
public/print/programs/tic.
University of Florida Center for School Improvement Teacher Inquiry. http://
education.ufl.edu/csi.

Publications

Caro-Bruce, C., Flessner, R., Klehr, M., & Zeichner, K. (2007). *Creating equitable classrooms through action research.* Thousand Oaks, CA: Corwin.

Cochran-Smith, M., & Lytle, S. L. (1993). *Inside/outside: Teacher research and knowledge.* New York: Teachers College Press.

Cochran-Smith, M., & Lytle, S. L. (1999). Relationships of knowledge and practice: Teacher learning in communities. *Review of Research in Education, 24,* 249–305.

Cochran-Smith, M., & Lytle, S. L. (2001). Beyond certainty: Taking an inquiry stance on practice. In A. Lieberman & L. Miller (Eds.), *Teachers caught in the action: Professional development that matters* (pp. 45–58). New York: Teachers College Press.

Cochran-Smith, M., & Lytle, S. L. (2009) *Inquiry as stance: Practitioner research for the next generation.* New York: Teachers College Press.

Dana, N. F. (2009). *Leading with passion and knowledge: The principal as action researcher.* Thousand Oaks, CA: Corwin.

Dana, N. F., & Yendol-Hoppey, D. (2008). *The reflective educator's guide to professional development: Coaching inquiry-oriented learning communities.* Thousand Oaks, CA: Corwin.

Dana, N. F., & Yendol-Hoppey, D. (2009). *The reflective educator's guide to classroom research: Learning to teach and teaching to learn through practitioner inquiry* (2nd ed.). Thousand Oaks, CA: Corwin.

9

Coaching Models

Peer, Culturally Responsive, and Content Focused

Peer coaching *can be a powerful alternative form of professional development for teachers; but to be successful, the relationship one develops with the peer-coaching partner is of critical importance. When it comes to peer coaching, questions are where it's at! A coach must be a skilled questioner to help the coached teacher both clarify and reflect on practice.*

—Deirdre Bauer, Radio Park Elementary School Principal

In culturally responsive coaching, *we can't make assumptions about the students or the adults. Do not assume that because a child has come from a "poor" background that they are unhappy, unintelligent, or their needs are not being met at home. Do not assume that even though a teacher may come from the same background as the students they are teaching, the teacher necessarily knows how to interact with or teach the kids. Culturally responsive coaching reminds us to never make assumptions and always be respectful of where people have come from and the experiences they have had. Through respectful, positive, constructive, and explicit coaching in best practices, we are most successful in retaining teachers in our high-needs schools. Culturally responsive coaching is a tool that addresses the often-unspoken complexities of teaching that remain hidden deep within one's teaching practice.*

—Lauren Gibbs, Coach and University Field Advisor

Content-focused coaching *is the most-powerful sustained professional development we have implemented to support teachers as they evolve and improve mathematics and science instructional practices. The coaches are a resource for the teachers; the teacher-coach team can work together to better meet the individual learning needs of the students.*

—Mary Lynn Westfall,
East Fairmont High School Teacher and Coach

Coaching is indeed a powerful professional development tool to add to our toolbox. Deirdre's, Lauren's, and Mary Lynn's reflections on their coaching experiences suggest a spectrum of activities that fall under the coaching umbrella. Like inquiry, coaching is a tool that can cultivate all three types of knowledge—*for, in,* and *of* practice. What coaching adds to our toolbox is a one-to-one professional relationship with another educator focused on reaching a specified goal. By working together, the coaching dyad systematically studies how to develop and integrate new knowledge into teaching.

In Chapter 9, we explore three different coaching models that help educators integrate external knowledge from the research literature while simultaneously creating internal knowledge that strengthens and sustains new practices: peer coaching, content-focused coaching, and culturally responsive coaching. These are just three of the models available to educators interested in transferring their new professional knowledge to their daily teaching practices.

DEFINITION: COACHING

Given the number and variation of coaching positions emerging on the educational terrain, one might wonder, what is coaching? Coaching is a professional development tool that educators use to learn from and with one another. Common components of the coaching process include a sequence of steps. In step one, establishing readiness, the coach and teacher share with each other their beliefs about teaching and learning within a context of trust and support. In step two, the preconference, the teacher identifies an area that she would like to explore within the lesson she will be teaching. The power of the preconference is that the conversation allows the teacher to guide the coach's gaze to an area of perceived need or felt difficulty, and the two collaboratively decide the type of data to be collected in the observation. Once the teacher and the coach enter step three, teaching observation, the coach captures observation data related to what the teacher wished to gain insights into about her teaching. Upon completion of the observation, the coach and the teacher engage in a postconference by reviewing the data, discussing the meaning and implications of the data, and setting goals for future teaching efforts. Given that this is a cycle, the process then repeats itself. Although each of the coaching models we explore in this chapter use a similar cycle, nuances exist between them that allow educators to target specific areas of need within one's teaching practices.

Peer Coaching

Peer coaching is a tool that encourages learning conversations between colleagues. The process allows colleagues to consult with one another, observe one another, and discuss teaching practices in a way that promotes collegiality, support, and student learning. Typically, two teachers work together to refine their practice in a nonthreatening way that allows them to learn and grow together. Peer coaching is typically used when teachers are trying to infuse the same teaching practice into their instructional repertoire or one peer has already incorporated the teaching practice into his or her repertoire, and his or her peer is interested in developing similar expertise.

Culturally Responsive Coaching

Culturally responsive coaching helps teachers identify ways to value, respect, and honor diverse backgrounds and ethnicities within their classrooms as well as examine deeply one's own equity-oriented beliefs. The model was created by blending the more general coaching approaches with the concept of cultural responsiveness and utilizes a planning conversation, a reflecting conversation, and a problem solving conversation to explore equity issues that emerge within the classroom. Culturally responsive coaching is important to use when teachers believe that issues of culture or equity may be inhibiting student learning within their school and classroom.

Content-Focused Coaching

Content-focused coaching is designed to promote student learning as educators plan, deliver, and reflect together on their development and implementation of standards-based instruction in a content area. This can be done with another teacher who is a specialist in the content area or another content-area expert. Since the focus is on a particular content area, the teacher works jointly with a knowledgeable content specialist to develop both content knowledge and pedagogical content knowledge. As you recall, in Chapter 1, we discussed the complexity of professional knowledge and Lee Shulman's (1987a, 1987b) work about the importance of developing pedagogical content knowledge for student learning to occur. Content-focused coaching specifically helps teachers at all career levels cultivate this sophisticated blending of context, students, content, pedagogy, and curriculum knowledge to create pedagogical content knowledge.

You will enjoy seeing the variety of coaching models available to you and this variety will help you understand why you must carefully select your coaching approach in order to meet a specific professional learning need. We also want you to know that there are many more models available, and you should expand your coaching knowledge beyond these three (some are referenced at the end of the chapter).

ILLUSTRATION: PEER-COACHING

To illustrate how the coaching plays out as a job-embedded, professional development tool, we eavesdrop on Ann and Carol, who have decided to engage in peer coaching.

On a hot, sunny day in late July, Ann and Carol met for lunch at a local restaurant. They had been teaching the same high school science courses at a large urban high school in Florida for years and had spent a week during the summer in workshops that focused on cultivating higher-level thinking skills and problem-based learning in the content areas. The workshop had stirred up some new ideas as well as professional dilemmas, and they were anxious to begin planning together for the year ahead.

Carol began,

> I remember so much of high school as being boring—*drill and kill* was how I affectionately referred to many of my school experiences. I think it's really important to engage learners. The things I liked most about my high school science experiences were the engaging things we did. Even though that is what I want my teaching to look like, I am not sure I am doing that. There are so many management issues when I try more hands-on, problem-based science instruction. If I can't get beyond management concerns, class won't be engaging, and they won't learn. I feel like much of what we learned in the workshop I just won't be able to figure out.

Ann responded,

> I agree that it is important to engage students. I've been struggling a bit with finding the balance between assuring that my students really understand the content and engaging my students. I'd like to use peer coaching to help us follow up on the workshop. I think that if we commit the time to coaching, we will figure this out together.

Carol and Ann agreed and began working together. Their first step was to decide when they would meet. They began by meeting with the principal and assistant principal to identify a way to embed this type of collaboration in their school day. At the meeting, they explained the purpose, process, and importance of working together to implement the new knowledge they had gained at the summer workshop. They also outlined the type of data that they would share from their peer-coaching efforts at the conclusion of their collaboration. The focus on data really seemed to help them gain buy in and support from the administrative team at their school.

During this preconference, they asked, "How can we be sure that our students really understand the content as we shift to more engaging instruction?" Carol and Ann set up a meeting time to plan the first observation lesson together and a date to observe the lesson as well as a time at the end of that day to talk about the observation. Carol suggested, "When we conference before the observation, we can decide the ways we might collect data for each other. This could give us insights into our questions. We can explore the data together in our postobservation conference."

Two days later, Ann and Carol met before school to discuss Carol's lesson on chemical reactions. Ann started the preconference by asking Carol which skills she planned to teach, what the lesson objectives included, what management issues she envisioned might compromise the lesson, how she was going to be proactive in setting up a successful lesson, what data should be collected, and what materials she would need. The preconference established that Ann would collect anecdotal data as well as a time-on-task chart to determine the level of student engagement in the lesson, and Carol agreed to collect the student work that they would collaboratively analyze after the lesson to identify the degree of student learning that occurred.

During sixth period, Carol began her lesson, and Ann sat next to a student, observing and keeping track of on-task behavior using a class-seating chart. At five minute intervals, Ann did a sweep of the entire classroom and noted the behavior of each learner in every lab group using a key: "A" stood for active listening and was used during the whole group instruction; and "ON" stood for on-task behavior, with "OT" referring to off-task behavior during the group component. Periodically, Ann visited the student groups and asked them probing questions about what they were learning. She recorded their responses. Before ending the lesson, Carol collected the student lab sheets and gave them to Ann to review before their discussion.

Carol was looking forward to the postconference observation after school. During the postconference, Ann began by asking Carol about how she thought the lesson went and what changes she would make in the future. Ann didn't want to tell Carol what she thought should change in the lesson. Rather, Carol's self-reflection was what Ann was interested in hearing. As Carol talked, Ann listened and learned a lot more about teaching the lesson she observed. She periodically asked probing and clarifying questions. Eventually, the conversation naturally shifted to the data collected as Ann and Carol looked at the chart to see when the students were most engaged and which students appeared to be consistently less engaged. Together, they reflected on the data and shared insights about what they saw. Ann asked questions that made Carol really think about her teaching differently than she had before.

During the conference, they also analyzed the student work for concept attainment and talked about the anecdotal records from the group observations. When Carol interpreted the data, she realized that when she had the students use technology and gave them specific short-term tasks, the students were highly engaged and demonstrated understanding of the concepts. However, they still had difficulties moving to the more abstract use of the concept within the group work. This led to further questions related to concept attainment and application to be explored in future coaching cycles. The conference really provided Carol and Ann the time to slow down and discuss instruction in data-driven ways.

When Ann and Carol were finished with the postconference, Ann asked Carol about her experience with the coaching cycle. She told Ann that the process made her feel more curious about her teaching, and the cycle allowed her to feel as if they were working more closely together on important concerns about student learning. At the end of their discussion, Carol and Ann made plans for Carol to observe Ann the following week, and together they identified their new question for investigation.

As the cycle progressed, Carol and Ann collaboratively explored many new science strategies and materials they found on Web sites and in professional journals. These strategies became new regularities in the classroom as Ann and Carol recognized their merit and embraced them. The data that was collected through each coaching cycle was also beneficial for their goal of enhancing student engagement. The data they gathered led Carol and Ann to better understand how their students experienced multiple learning activities and how the professional development activities eventually influenced their students' attitudes and understanding of science. An exciting outcome of their partnership was that Ann and Carol shared their learning about student engagement with colleagues at a faculty meeting at the end of the school year.

ILLUSTRATION: CULTURALLY RESPONSIVE COACHING

School districts interested in addressing systemic school practices that contribute to disproportion in special education or wanting to identify challenges associated with closing the achievement gap between subgroups often provide coaches who work with teachers to heighten their awareness of culture and race in schools.

The support described, referred to as culturally responsive coaching, uses this same process that Ann and Carol engaged in throughout the school year. Let's visit Ann and Carol's coaching work during the following school year.

Ann and Carol each realized that their work toward engaging students was making a difference but still realized they were missing a subset of children in their classroom. As a result, they requested help from David, one of the building coaches who was familiar with culturally responsive teaching. They agreed that culturally responsive teaching was the focus, prior to entering the coaching cycle, and that the coach's role would be to help them develop knowledge *for, in,* and *of* practice related to culturally responsive teaching.

David began his work as coach by providing opportunities for Ann and Carol to create knowledge for practice related to culturally responsive teaching practices. He suggested that Ann and Carol participate with the faculty in a book study using the text *Courageous Conversations About Race* (2005) by Glenn Singleton and Cutis Linton and process their learning during the book study using protocols as conversation tools to explore effective strategies for closing the achievement gap in their schools.

Once they collaboratively selected strategies they wanted to test out, the coaching dyads (David and Carol, and David and Ann) focused on implementing and studying their progress toward culturally responsive classroom practice using the same process described in the peer-coaching example. By the end of the cycle, Ann and Carol could both identify shifts in their teaching and increased engagement by some of the students they had been concerned about not reaching in their classroom.

ILLUSTRATION: CONTENT-FOCUSED COACHING

Our third illustration focuses on content-focused coaching. Like other coaching models, content-focused coaching is designed to develop the knowledge, skills, and abilities that help a teacher become and remain well equipped to help all students succeed in the content area. We are referring to content-focused coaching broadly, and some examples would include math coaching, reading coaching, literacy coaching, science coaching, and social studies coaching. Let's visit with a content-focused coaching dyad that has agreed to investigate mathematics instruction:

> We began by recognizing that teachers in our building would need support as we shifted to a new mathematics text. The approach used in the text was much more interactive and conceptual than

our last text. We also knew that in order to implement the math curriculum, we would need to all understand not just the surface-level changes but also explore the conceptual changes that we knew were present but needed to spend time cultivating as a part of our teaching practice.

Working individually with each teacher on the team, John, the math coach, helped each teacher identify a guiding question that tied together inquiry into mathematics content, mathematics instruction, and student learning.

Once the question was selected, the coach and teacher began the coaching cycle previously described, consulting with one another, observation, and discussing mathematics teaching practices that would enhance student learning. Like peer coaching, the content-focused coaching process is a job-embedded, professional development practice that brings coaches with a particular expertise together with classroom teachers to design, implement, and reflect on rigorous, standards-based lessons that promote student learning. Similar to culturally responsive coaching, an agreement is made by the teacher and coach to focus on a particular subject area.

WHAT HAVE WE LEARNED?

Coaching is a very flexible process and open to negotiation between the coach and the teacher. As you hear in these coaches' voices, coaching helped transform teaching and learning. Table 9.1 indicates that when you use coaching, the process attends to each of the professional knowledge building blocks. Peer coaching, as well as other coaching models such as content-focused coaching and culturally responsive coaching, use similar processes but have very specific lenses and often focus specifically on exploring and building knowledge related to a specific area.

Before concluding, we want to recognize that coaching is not a new form of professional development. In fact, twenty-seven years ago, Bruce Joyce and Beverly Showers (1983), leaders in the field of professional development research, provided educators with the following statistical support for coaching:

Five percent of learners will transfer a new skill into their practice as a result of theory.

Ten percent will transfer a new skill into their practice with theory and demonstration.

Twenty percent will transfer a new skill into their practice with theory and demonstration, and practice within the training.

Table 9.1   Coaching: Building Blocks for Powerful Professional Learning

Building-Block Type	Building Blocks						Theorists
Learning Needs	Understanding of research-based practice	View model	Practice time	Feedback and Coaching	Collaborative conversation and reflection		Borko (2004); Desimone (2009); Joyce and Showers (1983)
Orientation	Outside orientation			Inside orientation			Marzano, Pickering, and Pollock (2001); Cochran-Smith and Lytle (1999, 2001, 2009)
Type of Knowledge	Pedagogical knowledge	Curriculum knowledge	Student knowledge	Content knowledge	Context knowledge	Pedagogical content knowledge	Grossman (1990); Magnusson, Krajcik, and Borko (1999); Shulman (1987a, 1987b)
Source of Knowledge	Knowledge for practice		Knowledge in practice		Knowledge of practice		Cochran-Smith and Lytle (1999, 2001, 2009)

Twenty-five percent will transfer a new skill into their practice with theory and demonstration, practice within the training, and feedback.

Ninety percent will transfer a new skill into their practice with theory and demonstration, practice within the training, feedback, and coaching.

These statistics clearly highlight the value that the coaching process adds to enhancing teaching practice.

SOME THINGS TO THINK ABOUT

- *What is the degree of comfort that exists with these tools at your school?*

Each member of the coaching dyad must demonstrate a willingness to take calculated risks with their teaching as they move out of isolation to make their professional work public. Coaching typically involves two educators who possess a relationship built on mutual respect, confidentiality, and trust that supports an inquiry orientation. Comfort with these coaching models will require a movement of teachers out of isolation by developing a one-on-one professional relationship that focuses on enhancing teacher learning and student performance.

- *How ready is your school's culture to implement the tools?*

Coaching thrives within a culture that is ready for collaboration and dedicated to learning. One of our colleagues, Jim Nolan, says that all teachers should be expected to grow professionally—it is how they grow professionally that they must have a choice in shaping. As you can see in Carol and Ann's collaboration, coaching is a tool that they believed helped them grow. It was a learning tool rather than an evaluation tool. There must be a clear distinction within your school between coaching and evaluation. Additionally, schools that have a culture of trust, where teachers have respect for one another, will facilitate the introduction of this work. By defining the role and work of coaches as support rather than evaluation, this distinction becomes apparent to teachers.

- *How would you carve out time to use these tools in your building?*

A rotating substitute is one way to free up teachers to engage in peer coaching. Deirdre Bauer, principal at Radio Park Elementary School in State College, Pennsylvania, has also covered classes herself to free up teachers to engage in peer coaching. Planning periods can also be utilized by teachers and coaches to engage in pre- and postconference discussions.

- *What resources would you need to successfully use these tools?*

The greatest resources needed to implement the coaching models will be release time for peer coaching during the instructional day and educators who have content and cultural proficiency. Many districts have hired teachers as full-time coaches to provide the support we have discussed. However, remember that without creating a learning culture within the school that values and provides time for this type of job-embedded learning, it is unlikely that the human resources dedicated to encouraging learning will reap the learning benefits desired.

- *What type of data might you collect while using these tools?*

Like teacher inquiry, data collection and analysis is a naturally occurring activity within the coaching cycle. The goal will be to identify data-collection tools that can be used during the observation to capture activity related to the research question. Additionally, the examination of student work will be essential to a successful coaching cycle. In Chapter 11, we explore many different types of data-collection strategies that can be integrated into the coaching cycle.

ADDITIONAL RESOURCES

Web Sites

Literacy Coaching Clearinghouse. http://www.literacycoachingonline.org.
Peer Coaching for Improvement of Teaching and Learning. http://www.teachnet.org/TNPI/research/growth/becker.htm.
School Improvement Network, PD 360. http://www.pd360.com/pd360.cfm?.

Publications

Allen, D. W., & Le Blanc, A. C. (2005). *Collaborative peer coaching that improves instruction.* Thousand Oaks, CA: Corwin.

Corwin. (2008). *Mentoring, coaching, and collaboration.* Thousand Oaks, CA: Author.

Jacobs, J. L. (2007, February 24). *Coaching for equity: Meeting the needs of diverse learners through field supervision.* Paper presented at the annual meeting of the American Association of Colleges for Teacher Education, New York. Retrieved December 6, 2009, from http://www.allacademic.com/meta/p142691_index.html.

Jay, A. B., & Stong, M. W. (2008). *A guide to literacy coaching: Helping teachers increase student achievement.* Thousand Oaks, CA: Corwin.

Killion, J., & Harrison, C. (2006). Taking the lead: New roles for teachers and school-based coaches. Oxford, OH: National Staff Development Council.

Knight, J. (2007). *Instructional coaching: A partnership approach to improving instruction.* Thousand Oaks, CA: Corwin.

Knight, J. (2009). *Coaching: Approaches and perspectives.* Thousand Oaks, CA: Corwin.

Lindsey, D. B., Martinez, R. S., & Lindsey, R. B. (2007). *Culturally proficient coaching: Supporting educators to create equitable schools.* Thousand Oaks, CA: Corwin.

Morse, A. (2009). *Cultivating a math coaching practice: A guide for K–8 math educators.* Thousand Oaks, CA: Corwin.

West, L. (2002). *Content-focused coaching: Transforming mathematics lessons.* Thousand Oaks, CA: Corwin.

Yendol-Hoppey, D., & Dana, N. F. (2007). *The reflective educator's guide to mentoring: Strengthening practice through knowledge, story, and metaphor.* Thousand Oaks, CA: Corwin.

10

Professional Learning Communities

The learning community *work at our school provided the faculty and me, as principal, with the structure to make professional development more meaningful, efficient, and focused on students. We learned protocols to use depending on the situation or problem being studied. Our learning communities frequently focused on student work, helping us evaluate student learning and then redesign lessons to improve achievement for our students. With the purpose always focused on improving student learning, our students benefited greatly from our learning-community conversations.*

—Kathy Dixon, Williams Elementary School Principal

Our work in creating inclusive schools is complex. It requires teachers and administrators working together to shift ideas. We examine beliefs, read together, visit other schools, create action plans, try "out and on" inclusive practices, and make data-based decisions. The process moves back and forth between examining inside and outside teacher knowledge. Without working in community, *there is little pressure and support to make difficult and lasting changes in schools.*

—David Hoppey, Alachua County Special Education Supervisor

These educators' insights demonstrate how a professional learning community is a tool that functions as a kind of job-embedded learning container. Professional learning communities (PLCs) come in all shapes and sizes, and educational consultants and authors across the country are creating processes and procedures, steps and rules to guide professional learning communities that differ in somewhat substantial ways. However, a common feature of all PLC work is that PLCs integrate a number of the job-embedded learning strategies discussed previously in Part II. For this reason, we saved the professional learning community as the final tool to discuss in Part II of this book.

The purpose of this final chapter in Part II is not to define and differentiate the many iterations of the PLC concept. Rather, we focus on our work with teachers and administrators in schools, which has encouraged us to take a broad and practitioner-driven definition of professional learning community, one that allows educators not only to participate in the process but also to have a say in the development of the PLC process at their school. The overarching description of a successful PLC is simple—have robust conversations about improving teaching and learning that include research, multiple forms of data, teacher knowledge construction, and public sharing that target and ultimately lead to improved student learning. So, what makes a professional learning community a professional learning community?

DEFINITION: PROFESSIONAL LEARNING COMMUNITY

We looked across the various models of PLCs to find some commonalities. PLCs are typically groups of six to twelve educators who connect and network with each other through collaborative dialogue about their teaching practice. PLCs meet on a regular basis, and their time together is often structured by the use of processes, steps, or protocols to ensure focused, deliberate dialogue by teachers about student work and student learning (Dana & Yendol-Hoppey, 2008; DuFour, 2004; Hord, 1997). The professional dialogue is targeted at changing teaching practice to enhance student learning.

Online PLCs and social networks are professional development vehicles that can provide flexibility to PLCs. By connecting teachers to one another online, they can communicate with one another about teaching and learning in an asynchronous timeframe. Utilizing digital tools, teachers can develop a professional learning network that supports them both professionally and personally.

ILLUSTRATION: INQUIRY-ORIENTED PLC

The illustration provided is of an inquiry-oriented PLC that takes place in an elementary school where Kurt Thomas, the math coach, meets during a shared fourth- and fifth-grade planning period with six elementary teachers each Tuesday for one hour. The learning community work is driven by Kurt and his community members' identification of student needs and resulting teacher learning needs, the important rules for a professional learning community (e.g., robust conversations about improving teaching and learning that include research, multiple forms of data, teacher knowledge construction, and public sharing that target and ultimately lead to improved student learning), and the PLC members' collective, systematic attention to their job-embedded learning. Let's eavesdrop on their learning community at work.

Before beginning PLC work, this group of teachers' planning period was characterized by a focus on logistical features of teaching such as planning upcoming events and completing paperwork. The meeting was more like a committee than a context for professional learning. In order to reculture the orientation toward professional learning within the school building, the principal and team leaders decided to adjust the schedule to allow a ninety-minute planning period. During this period, grade-level teams would commit to spending sixty minutes engaged in collaborative learning each week. In addition to dedicating time to learning, the principal worked with her faculty to redesign their yearly alternative evaluation tool to emphasize teachers documenting their professional learning and student learning. These structural shifts set the stage for a culture of professional learning to emerge within the school.

Given that Kurt recognized the importance and potential difficulty of shifting the use of the planning period from logistics to learning, he began by working with his colleagues to help them understand the concept of a professional learning community. To these ends, Kurt introduced a reading by DuFour (2004) during their first August meeting and the group engaged in a text-based discussion using a National School Reform Faculty (NSRF) protocol (http://www.nsrfharmony.org). The dialogue that emerged as a result of this text-based discussion helped the team envision what this new orientation toward learning could look like and what their responsibility would be.

The following week, the group moved toward defining an area of shared interest, which they could explore within the learning community. Knowing that students were not doing well on the state mathematics exam, the group chose to focus on understanding what the difficulty might be for their students in mathematics. During the first thirty minutes of the gathering, the group examined several student-data sources using the NSRF protocol "Looking at Patterns in Student Work" (http://www.nsrfharmony.org/protocol/learning_from_student_work.html). The data conversation revealed a shared concern about the students' progress in mathematics. This data indicated that the bottom and top quartile students were not making the desired progress.

Although the group had recently engaged in a series of differentiated-instruction workshops and implemented a new mathematics curriculum with fidelity, the students seemed to have differentiated success rates. As a result of these concerns, this PLC decided to explore ways of differentiating mathematics instruction and the curriculum to meet all learners' needs. This process of collaboratively examining data allowed the group to identify a shared purpose for working together.

Interestingly, although many of the teachers on this team had participated in traditional differentiated-instruction workshops during the previous year, few of the teachers felt confident in their ability to implement differentiated instruction within their classrooms. Applying differentiated-instruction strategies required them to adjust how they grouped students, how students learn new material, and how students could best present the information they had learned (Tomlinson, 1999). Because this method takes time and practice to master, they believed that collaboration could strengthen teachers' use of differentiation. During the next few weeks, the teachers deepened their collaboration efforts by engaging in at least one peer observation of a colleague's mathematics instruction using the protocols found on the NSRF Web site (http://www.nsrfharmony.org/protocol/school_visits.html).

As October began, Kurt and his community collaboratively identified a variety of tools that could deepen the group's work. During the first meeting of the month, Kurt realized that the teachers needed to review what differentiation meant and develop an image of what differentiated instruction looked like in classrooms. They identified one of Carol Tomlinson's (1999), books, *The Differentiated Classroom,* and began a book study that helped teachers begin to discuss with each other how this new knowledge could be applied to their classrooms. Over the course of the year, Kurt continued the external knowledge thread by bringing in guests who were knowledgeable about differentiated instruction to speak with the group. By building on knowledge introduced at a districtwide inservice presentation the previous year and bringing in new knowledge from external sources, Kurt and his community acknowledged the importance of knowledge *for* practice while simultaneously realizing that they must make sure there are opportunities at other PLC meetings for teachers to move beyond the processing of disseminated information to engage in real and meaningful change in the classroom.

During the following meeting, Kurt attended to the teachers' needs to engage in real and meaningful change in the classroom. To these ends, he once again created the opportunity for teachers to examine the kind of math work that their students were currently engaged in as well as get a sense of the learning that was and was not occurring. Kurt introduced some new protocols into the learning community created by the NSRF (http://www.nsrfharmony.org/protocol/looking_work.html) that facilitated looking at student work from their own classrooms. By examining their own students' work, the PLC members deepened their knowledge of the students' strengths and weaknesses, the strengths and weaknesses of their curriculum, and their own planning. The teachers' collective focus on student work also helped shift the group toward a culture of professional learning characterized by open, honest, and thoughtful conversation.

During the next month of PLC meetings, Kurt wanted to move the group beyond looking at student work to raising questions about their own teaching practices. Kurt asked teachers to bring dilemmas of practice associated with their early attempts at differentiation and the changes they had made as a result of examining the student work. Over the course of the year, the group used many protocols created by the NSRF (http://www .nsrfharmony.org/protocol/learning_dilemmas.html) to facilitate these conversations and help the PLC members dialogue about ways to resolve these dilemmas of practice.

Finally, during one of the meetings in November, Kurt suggested that the group turn their gaze toward teacher inquiry, also known as action research. He began the meeting by presenting the action-research process and sharing an example of his own action research. As a part of this next meeting, each teacher crafted a subquestion that connected to the overarching, teacher-generated, shared-inquiry question, "How do we differentiate mathematics instruction to meet all learners' needs?" For example, Jason, a fifth-grade classroom teacher, and Sara, the special education teacher who spends the entire ninety-minute mathematics block coteaching in Jason's classroom two days each week, elected to study, "How does coteaching allow teachers to differentiate math instruction for their students?" and "What happens to student learning as a result of our coteaching?" Other teachers inquired into individual questions related to differentiation in mathematics such as, "How does differentiating my assessment tools influence student learning?" and "How do I adjust mathematics-curriculum content to meet the needs of struggling learners without lowering expectations for success?" Although the subquestions held by individual teachers within this PLC differed, the entire PLC was committed to supporting each other's inquiry and student growth in the area of mathematics.

Over the course of the PLC meetings held through December, the teachers each generated a plan for their action research that contained the purpose of their research, the guiding question or wondering, how data would be collected and analyzed, and a tentative timeline for the project's completion. During this time, all teachers developed and received feedback on plans for their individual or shared research around questions that differed somewhat but all related to the common theme of differentiated mathematics instruction. Later PLC activities supported the other phases of the inquiry process. For example, some meetings focused on each member of the PLC sharing and analyzing the data they collected as a part of their action research using a protocol from *The Reflective Educator's Guide to Professional Development: Coaching Inquiry-Oriented Learning Communities* (Dana & Yendol-Hoppey, 2008). The group realized that one of the key attributes of the inquiry process was that they focus on gathering and analyzing data that could serve as evidence of changes in teacher and student learning. Discussing their data-analysis process with PLC members allowed the teachers to self-analyze whether the changes they were making actually made a difference.

The duration of the year was spent moving in and out of these various activities based on the group's articulated needs. For example, some meetings would be dedicated to various components of the action-research process while other meetings were used to examine student work, resolve dilemmas, debrief classroom observations, engage in lesson study, and incorporate external knowledge into the group through readings and guest presentations. By the end of the school year, all but one of the teachers in this PLC demonstrated changes in practice and celebrated noteworthy student gains in both their lower and top quartile students. The remaining teacher, who was resistant to the shift in professional learning demands, demonstrated some superficial changes in practice with only modest student-learning gains.

WHAT HAVE WE LEARNED?

Professional learning communities are spaces or "containers" (Easton, 2008) for job-embedded professional development within schools. These containers create the metaphorical back porch that brings teachers and administrators together to systematically integrate each of the tools described in Part II, as well as many others not explored in this book. The integration of these tools into professional learning at your school has the power to improve teaching and learning. In many ways, PLCs place the onus of the responsibility for professional learning on those closest to the students—teachers and administrators. With this responsibility also comes accountability. This accountability will require that we are not only mindful of all the professional knowledge building blocks (presented in Table 10.1) needed to plan job-embedded professional learning but we are also prepared to make our efforts public.

If we want to get the "biggest bang for our buck" from professional development, allowing educators to work in community within their school walls is essential. However, change and buy in to the concept of working in community takes time to develop. Not all teachers will embrace the concept from the start. Staff developers, teacher leaders, and administrators need to have patience as teachers shift their ways of working with one another, realizing that reluctant or resistant teachers may make only modest changes, if any, in their teaching practice through professional learning community work. As learning in community becomes the norm at a school, however, reluctance and resistance diminish over time, and professional learning and growth for all teachers can flourish.

Table 10.1 PLCs: Building Blocks for Powerful Professional Learning

Building-Block Type	Building Blocks						Theorists
Learning Needs	Understanding of research-based practice		View model	Practice time	Feedback and Coaching	Collaborative conversation and reflection	Borko (2004); Desimone (2009); Joyce and Showers (1983)
Orientation	Outside orientation			Inside orientation			Marzano, Pickering, and Pollock (2001); Cochran-Smith and Lytle (1999, 2001, 2009)
Type of Knowledge	Pedagogical knowledge	Curriculum knowledge	Student knowledge	Content knowledge	Context knowledge	Pedagogical content knowledge	Grossman (1990); Magnusson, Krajcik, and Borko (1999); Shulman (1987a, 1987b)
Source of Knowledge	Knowledge for practice		Knowledge in practice		Knowledge of practice		Cochran-Smith and Lytle (1999, 2001, 2009)

SOME THINGS TO THINK ABOUT

- *What is the degree of comfort that exists with these tools at your school?*

To build the PLC in a way that actually leads to job-embedded learn-ing, we highly suggest that you engage your faculty in learning about, thinking about, and shaping the way to create job-embedded learning at your school. Buy in is critical from the PLC participants. Additionally, if this type of job-embedded learning is new to your school, be sure that the school leadership feels comfortable with sharing responsibility for teacher learning with the teachers themselves.

- *How ready is your school's culture to implement the tool?*

Given that teacher and administrator collaboration is central to PLC success, understanding and developing relationships that support profes-sional learning is important. The kind of culture that best supports job-embedded learning of this type is one characterized as collegial. Collegial contexts typically possess the following characteristics:

- Establishing and maintaining a vision
- Building trust
- Harnessing power to positively influence group dynamics
- Enhancing collaboration
- Recognizing the importance of diversity
- Becoming critical friends
- Documenting learning to keep the group accountable
- Gaining comfort with change
- Using data to inform work
- Building connections with school leadership

- *How would you carve out time to use these tools in your building?*

By turning over the responsibility and accountability for professional learning, districts and school leadership are not excused from guiding profes-sional development. School leadership will be instrumental in assuring that the necessary time exists to support this work. One way that those outside the school can help is by facilitating the exploration of new bell schedules that provide learning time for teachers during the day. School boards could recon-sider how they allot professional learning time in the school calendar. Title I, II, and VI money can be used in new and innovative ways to support the development of professional learning communities within the school day.

- *What resources would you need to successfully use these tools?*

In turning over the responsibility and accountability for professional learning, school and district leadership will also need to identify ways to build teacher leadership and knowledge of these, and other, job-embedded, professional development tools. Skilled teacher leaders, whether coaches or classroom teachers, will make or break the nature, scope, and success of professional learning communities.

- *What type of data might you collect while using these tools?*

As indicated throughout this chapter, PLCs rely on robust conversations about improving teaching and learning that include research, multiple forms of data, teacher knowledge construction, and public sharing that target and ultimately lead to improved student learning. Multiple forms of data would include everything from high-stakes testing to teacher observations of children in the classroom. The broader the use of data, the more likely that teachers will understand the complexity of the problems they are addressing. Chapter 11 will provide a more in-depth look at data and the role it plays in job-embedded professional learning.

ADDITIONAL RESOURCES

Web Sites

National Staff Development Council, Learning Communities. http://www .nsdc.org/standards/learningcommunities.cfm.

SEDL, *Professional Learning Communities: What Are They And Why Are They Important?* http://www.sedl.org/change/issues/issues61.html.

Solution Tree. http://www.solution-tree.com/Public/Main.aspx; http://www .allthingsplc.info/about/aboutPLC.php.

Publications

Clauset, K. H., Lick, D. W., & Murphey, C. U. (2009). *Schoolwide action research for professional learning communities: Improving student learning through the whole-faculty study groups approach.* Thousand Oaks, CA: Corwin.

Dana, N. F., & Yendol-Hoppey, D. (2008). *The reflective educator's guide to professional development: Coaching inquiry-oriented learning communities.* Thousand Oaks, CA: Corwin.

DuFour, R. (2004). What is a professional learning community? *Educational Leadership, 61*(8), 6–11.

Hord, S. M. (1997). *Professional learning communities: Communities of continuous inquiry and improvement.* Austin, TX: Southwest Educational Development Laboratory.

Roberts, S. M., & Pruitt, E. Z. (2009). *Schools as professional learning communities: Collaborative activities and strategies for professional development* (2nd ed.). Thousand Oaks, CA: Corwin.

Whitford, B. L., & Wood, D. (Eds.). (in press). *Teachers learning in community: Realities and possibilities.* Albany: State University of New York Press.

PART III

Using Your Toolbox

Tips for Developing a Successful Job–Embedded, Professional Development Program

N ow that you have added more tools to your job-embedded, professional development toolbox, you should feel ready to roll up your sleeves, open your toolbox, and begin planning how to use the tools to meet the professional learning needs of teachers at your school. Did you ever try to hammer a nail with a screwdriver? This usually doesn't work out so well. Choosing the wrong tool for the professional learning goal is equally self-defeating. Part III of this book is about matching the right tool with the right professional learning need. We imagine that although you are excited about all the tools at your disposal, you are still wondering, Where do I begin?

The last two chapters of this book will help you systematically and intentionally create a professional development plan that is powerful enough to change your practice as well as the practice of other educators with whom you work. Once you have created a plan, we will explore how to strengthen your plan by collecting data at each stage. This will allow you to provide evidence of instructional change as well as shifts in student learning over time. By collecting, organizing, analyzing, and sharing data related to your job-embedded, professional development efforts, you not only strengthen your learning but also acquire evidence that helps make the case for continued time and resources.

As with all innovations, we learn a lot by trying them out. Before closing the book, we share lessons we learned the hard way with the hope that you will plan to avoid these same dilemmas by being proactive. By the time you complete Part III, you should feel prepared to create your own job-embedded, professional development plan and feel familiar with the following concepts:

1. Matching professional development tools to needs using data

2. Creating a theory of change to guide your professional development work

3. Understanding factors that might influence your ability to make a perfect match for professional learning

4. Recognizing ten lessons learned that can help you plan, provide, and nurture job-embedded professional learning in your school

11

Making the Match

Aligning Data and the
Right Tools With Your Particular Needs

So far, we have explored two important tasks that will help you implement job-embedded learning in your school:

1. Assessing your own professional development needs as well as those of your teaching colleagues by considering the building blocks to powerful professional learning discussed in Part I and providing the necessary resources for successful implementation

2. Developing an array of strategies for your professional development toolbox that can help you develop a comprehensive school-based professional development plan

This chapter takes us a next step by helping us explore factors that you need to consider as you pair professional development strategies with your professional development need. Educators who make good matches will learn to accomplish more with less and garner a higher return rate on the staff-development matches they do make. Indeed, by making a good match, we save precious resources and actualize real change.

WHAT FACTORS SHOULD I CONSIDER
IN THE MATCHMAKING PROCESS?

We begin our discussion of matchmaking by looking across all the chapters in Part II of this book, which define and illustrate a variety of job-embedded, professional learning strategies: book studies, Webinars, podcasts, and online libraries; research-in-action and coteaching; conversation tools, such as protocols, open-space technology, and the knowledge café; lesson study; teacher inquiry; coaching; and professional learning communities, utilizing both face-to-face and online learning. One common theme unites them: All job-embedded, professional learning strategies incorporate the use of data.

This fact may not be intuitive at first glance if you are thinking of data in very traditional ways. In the current era of accountability, the most prevalent and noticeable data in many schools are quantitative measures of student achievement, and, in many schools, student performance on state tests becomes synonymous with the word *data*. Certainly, there is a lot that can be learned from student performance on tests, but there is a lot to be learned from a number of other data sources that may not be as obvious as the quantitative measures of student achievement that abound in today's schools.

Hence, an important factor to consider when making matches between professional development tools and professional development needs is to understand a number of different data collection techniques and draw upon these multiple techniques as part of job-embedded professional learning. Sources of data (other than quantitative measures of student achievement) include observations and field notes, student work, interviews, focus groups, digital pictures, video, reflective journals, Weblogs, and surveys. Savvy staff developers understand different forms of data and when to use them to inform how professional development unfolds over the course of a school year. Savvy staff developers match data collection strategies to learning needs in a school or district.

In addition, savvy staff developers match professional development strategies to the particular needs of their school or district, deciding which strategies should be used at what time and in what combination. Let's delve a bit deeper into these two sets of choices.

Factor One: Matching
Data Collection With Information Need

As a program of job-embedded professional learning unfolds over the course of the school year, intentional and systematic collection of data will help you measure the progress of teacher and student learning along the way. As previously mentioned, data collection is embedded in different ways in each professional development tool discussed in Part II of this book. To highlight the use of multiple types of data that can be used to assess progress toward teachers' knowledge construction, we will describe the ten most common strategies we have seen in connection with job-embedded professional learning.

Strategy 1: Observations and Field Notes

To capture "action" in the classroom, many teachers take field notes as they observe others or have someone field note their own teaching. Field notes can come in many shapes, forms, and varieties. Some of these include scripting dialog and conversation, diagramming the classroom or a particular part of the classroom, noting what a student or group of students are doing at particular time intervals (e.g., every two minutes), and recording every question that a teacher asks. Field notes are not interpretations but rather focus on capturing what is occurring without commenting as to why the action might be occurring or how one judges a particular act.

In addition to field notes, many other types of observation tools exist. For example, the Instructional Practice Inventory (IPI) created by Jerry Valentine (2009) allows teachers to engage in schoolwide observations of what is happening in classrooms to assess student engagement by observing instruction and creating profiles of schoolwide engagement and engaging faculty in discussions about instructional shifts that need to occur to reach schoolwide engagement goals. Our colleague, Lacy Redd remarked,

> The observation data took us to a new place in the way we worked together. We had a schoolwide focus and we had data from our own classrooms that caused a lot of great conversation between people who often don't even work together. I think we learned that collecting data can really help us take an honest look at what we are actually doing in our classrooms with children.

Those interested in data-driven observations will benefit by scouring educational venues for powerful observation tools that can capture teaching and learning as well as generate professional conversation.

Strategy 2: Documents, Artifacts, and Student Work

Schools and classrooms naturally generate a tremendous paper trail that captures much of the daily classroom activity. The paper trail includes student work; curriculum guides; textbooks; teacher manuals; children's literature; IEPs; district memos; parent newsletters; progress reports; teacher plan books; written lesson plans; and correspondence to and from parents, the principal, and specialists. When teaching and professional development are intertwined with one another, the papers become data and take on new meaning. Known as *artifacts,* systematically collected papers give you the opportunity to look within and across these documents to analyze them in new and different ways. For example, as a method of tracking student productivity in the classroom, many teachers save student work, stamping dates on the work to know when it was produced. Through looking at student work over time, claims can be made that could not occur when viewing a single piece of work.

Strategy 3: Interviews

Sometimes, interviewing is the best way to understand what is happening to teachers and students along the way. Interviewing can be informal and spontaneous or more thoughtfully planned. Depending on your focus, interviewing students in the classroom as well as interviewing adults, such as parents, administrators, other classroom teachers, and instructional support teachers, can be a rich source of data.

Strategy 4: Focus Groups

Focus groups offer teachers another vehicle for collecting the talk and thoughts of children in the classroom. In many ways, focus groups occur daily in the form of whole-class or small-group discussion. The focus-group discussion can serve as a tool for understanding students' perceptions. For example, a focus group can provide insight into how students experience a new instructional strategy. Although focus groups can serve as a quick way to obtain data, focus groups have some limitations. For example, focus groups are more likely to capture breadth of opinion because the goal is often to understand the group's perspective. In addition, sometimes due to the presence of diverging opinions, less confident focus-group members refrain from sharing their thoughts.

Strategy 5: Digital Pictures

Another wonderful way to capture action that occurs in the classroom as data is through digital photography. The digital pictures can serve two purposes—they document group progress over time and are also used to prompt during interviews.

Strategy 6: Video as Data

Video as a form of data collection takes digital pictures a step further by capturing an entire segment of action in the classroom over a set time period. Given that teachers often collect their best data by seeing and listening to the activities within their classroom, video becomes a powerful form of data collection.

Strategy 7: Reflective Journals

Capturing "thinking" is a challenge for any teacher. One way to capture the thinking that occurs in the school and classroom and within a teacher's own mind is through journaling. Journals provide teachers a tool for reflecting on their own thought processes and can also serve as a tool for students to record their thinking related to the project at hand.

Strategy 8: Weblogs

Similar to a journal, Weblogs are another excellent way teachers can capture their thinking as their teaching unfolds. Will Richardson (2006) defines Weblog in its most general sense as "an easily created, easily updateable Web site that allows an author (or authors) to publish instantly to the Internet from any Internet connection" (p. 17). As Weblogs consist of a series of entries arranged in reverse chronological order, they can serve as a sort of online diary where teachers can post commentary or news about the professional development they are currently engaged in. Unlike the journal as a form of data collection, the teacher who blogs can combine text, images, and links to other blogs as well as post comments in an interactive format. The comment feature of blogs provides the opportunity for educators to receive and record feedback.

Strategy 9: Surveys

Sometimes, more formal mechanisms to capture the action, talk, thinking, and productivity that are a part of each and every school day are needed. Surveys can give students a space to share their thoughts and opinions about a teaching technique or strategy, a unit, or their knowledge about particular subject matter.

Strategy 10: Quantitative Measures of Student Achievement
(Standardized Test Scores, Assessment Measures, and Grades)

As previously stated, in this era of high-stakes testing and accountability, numerous quantitative measures of student performance abound, and these measures are valuable sources of data.

Although this list of data sources is far from exhaustive, the list acknowledges how data comes in a variety of shapes and sizes. With systematic attention to the data-collection strategies you employ at each stage of professional development, you can help your efforts reap learning benefits for the adults and students in the schoolhouse. Select data-collection strategies that will best inform your work and be willing to make detours in your original job-embedded, professional development plan along the way if your data indicates the need for a new direction. In this way, data and planned job-embedded professional development become a match made in heaven.

Factor Two: Matching the Professional Development Tool With the Professional Development Need

You learned about a number of different strategies to actualize job-embedded professional development in Part II of this book. Many of these strategies become quite complex and intersect with one another. Yet, in Part II of this book, we presented them as separate entities so you could develop an "inventory" of a number of professional development tools. Only in Chapter 10, "Professional Learning Communities," did we begin to explicitly illustrate the way these tools can fit together. The savvy staff developer knows that the full value of these tools isn't realized by implementing the tools separately but by intentionally combining them and matching them to particular professional development needs in a district or school. To illustrate this match-making process, we turn to the story of a particular teacher leader, Keisha Wagner, and how she worked with various professional development tools to meet the needs of her sixth-grade language arts teaching team.

ILLUSTRATION: SIXTH-GRADE LANGUAGE ARTS TEACHER KEISHA WAGNER

Part One: Setting the Stage

Balancing her strong belief in interdisciplinary teaming with her belief that teachers who share the same discipline should have time to engage in discussion about their content, principal Tonya Brown organized her teachers into discipline-specific, grade-level teams that met during a common planning time once a week. She entrusted the professional development of her teachers to a team leader of each group. Each year, the team leader rotated so that all of the teachers were encouraged to develop teacher-leadership skills. One of her star teacher leaders was Keisha Wagner, who was the first selected to lead the sixth-grade language arts team.

Following her principal's creative scheduling, Keisha's team met during a common planning period each week. In September of the school year, Keisha led the group in the selection and articulation of a professional development goal. As teachers examined school reading and writing data, they recognized that bottom- and top-quartile students were not making the progress they desired in both reading and writing. As a result, they decided to explore ways to heighten their expectations for the top-quartile students as well as review the current curriculum used to meet the needs of the bottom-quartile learners.

Professional Development Need 1:
Become Knowledgeable About Reading
Strategies for Struggling Middle School Students

During the first meeting of the group, where they set their professional development goal, Keisha realized that the teachers needed to focus on one area at a time. They decided to explore the poor performance of the bottom-quartile readers first. Quickly, by looking at the comprehension data, the group realized that they were not sure what reading strategies and knowledge might really help these students. As a result, Keisha dug into her professional development toolbox and identified a variety of tools that could deepen their understanding of middle school reading instruction, particularly for struggling students. Keisha realized that the internal knowledge did not exist at their school, so she identified a book on literacy strategies titled *Classroom Strategies for Interactive Learning* by Doug Buehl (2001) and began a book study that helped teachers construct this new knowledge.

The group met for three weeks discussing the book, raising questions for each other, and providing ideas to each other about how the various strategies could reshape reading instruction during their Response to Intervention (RtI) supplemental period. After completing the book study, they also met with the school's RtI coach who provided them with the Web site for the Florida Center for Reading Research intervention database (http://www.fcrr.org) that the district had recently recognized as instrumental in facilitating teachers' knowledge of reading instruction.

Over the course of the year, Keisha continued the external-knowledge thread by bringing in guests from other schools, who were knowledgeable about embedding a variety of research-based tools into their instruction, for workshops. They also visited a few of the schools, including a visit to Research in Action at P. K. Yonge, that had made great progress with reading comprehension through the Florida Reading Initiative. By bringing in new knowledge from external sources, Keisha acknowledged the importance of knowledge *for* practice but simultaneously realized that she must make sure there are opportunities for teachers to move beyond processing disseminated information to engage in knowledge *in* and *of* practice that could enhance student reading performance.

Professional Development Need 2:
Become Knowledgeable About Students

During their second month of meetings, Keisha attended to the teachers' call for more inquiry into their own classroom reading instruction. To these ends, she created opportunities for teachers to examine student diagnostic assessments, discuss reading curriculum, share lesson plans, and present student work during their team meeting. This data analysis served as a catalyst for developing changes in their reading instruction. To structure this discussion, Keisha used a variety of the National School Reform Faculty protocols. For example, at a meeting in early October, the group used a protocol called The Slice (http://www.nsrfharmony.org/protocol/a_z.html).

The purpose of The Slice is to learn from examining all the student work produced during a narrow time period by a broad sample of students in a particular school. Being that the professional development topic was increasing reading comprehension in bottom-quartile learners, this sixth-grade team decided to collect the work that was produced during one class period of the RtI groups. This work created their sample. Keisha collected this work from each teacher in her team, removed from it all identifying names, and made a copy for each member of her team.

At their next meeting, Keisha began,

> So far, we have been focusing on learning more about reading comprehension strategies that could help our struggling readers. Today, we decided to focus on looking closely at work our own students have produced recently and analyze this work using the following guiding question: "Is class work appropriately challenging our bottom readers?" As you recall, we each collected student work produced during Wednesday's Response to Intervention lesson. I prepared all of that work, removing any identifying information, and placed it in your packet. We will now take the first 20 minutes of our meeting to examine this sample of student work in silence, and take notes on what we are noticing. At the end of 20 minutes, we will have a Socratic seminar discussion to debrief what we've learned from examining this "slice" of our students' work.

After twenty minutes, Keisha invited the teachers to discuss their notes. Together, the group realized from this examination a classic dilemma: Some of their bottom-quartile students were being inappropriately challenged, clearly leading to reading—specifically comprehension—frustration. This examination led teachers to realize they had a long way to go to actualize the comprehension strategies that they had been reading and observing. This particular meeting helped the teachers reaffirm their commitment to the goal of supporting these struggling readers, and they began to problem solve ways to pair the optimal level of challenge to each student, using the appropriate research-based strategy. The first step to doing so meant developing a more sophisticated set of tools for struggling middle school readers. By inquiring into their own student work through the use of protocols, these team members deepened their local knowledge of their students, their curriculum, and their own planning.

The group also concluded it was critical to gather evidence of improved student achievement across the school year to ensure students were learning and allow teachers to make instructional changes so interventions were responsive to student needs. Over the course of a few meetings, the team decided to use curriculum-based measures, such as student artifacts mentioned in The Slice protocol, in combination with regularly scheduled progress-monitoring probes that assess student learning every two weeks as evidence of student progress.

Professional Development Need 3: Deep Content Knowledge and Solving Dilemmas Emerging in the Classroom as Teachers Try New Reading Strategies

As a follow-up, Keisha asked teachers to bring dilemmas of practice associated with their early RtI reading efforts. Keisha introduced many protocols, such as the National School Reform Faculty's Consultancy protocol, to facilitate these conversations about ways to resolve these dilemmas of practice.

While all of these activities were in action, Keisha purposefully organized teachers to engage in peer observation and content-focused coaching as they tested out a variety of new reading curriculum and research-based strategies, which would ultimately create knowledge in practice and encourage dialogue about that activity that had the potential to generate knowledge of practice. Although peer observation focused on a content question was initially uncomfortable for teachers who rarely observed each other, over time it became a natural activity.

Professional Development Need 4: Become More Knowledgeable About Curriculum and Pedagogy

Once the group felt more comfortable working collaboratively, Keisha introduced the lesson study tool and the team worked together throughout the next few months to plan, observe, assess, and modify three research lessons. This led to some model Response to Intervention reading lessons that were even videotaped and shared outside this team with other grade-level teachers.

Professional Development Need 5: Gain Deeper Insight Into How the Strategies to Strengthen Reading Instruction Were Playing Out in Practice

Finally, Keisha turned the group's gaze toward action research. Spending the last few months of the year engaging in action research on the multiple forms of data they had collected throughout the school year as well as collecting and analyzing additional data allowed these educators the opportunity to synthesize and create all three sources of professional knowledge construction: knowledge *for* practice, knowledge *in* practice, and knowledge *of* practice. Each teacher within the learning community crafted a subquestion that connects to the overarching shared question, "How do we strengthen reading comprehension during Response to Intervention for our bottom-quartile readers?" For example, one teacher in the group, Mr. Johnson, and the inclusion teacher, who cotaught the intervention block to engage in action research, asked the question, "How does coteaching strengthen our ability to provide targeted curriculum?" Other teachers in the group inquired into individual questions, such as, "How do reading comprehension assessment tools influence my ability to address student-reading weaknesses?" As a group, they recommitted to supporting each other's growth and student growth in the area of reading comprehension during the remaining three months of the school year.

At the end of the school year, they shared the results of their action-research studies at a faculty meeting, generating interest from other colleagues at their middle school in the curriculum, research-based strategies, coteaching, and assessment tools that can be used to strengthen reading comprehension for struggling sixth-grade readers.

This illustration provides us an image of what job-embedded professional learning looks like. In each of the activities—book study, student-work examination, dilemma investigation, coaching, lesson study, action research, and others—these educators shared a question that focused their collaborative work: "How do we increase reading comprehension for our bottom-quartile students during Response to Intervention?" This theme and guiding question gave content and purpose to their collective work. As you can see, commingling these job-embedded, professional development tools creates knowledge for, in, and of practice as teachers collaborate during their school day.

Keisha and her team selected some of the different strategies from Part II of this book to meet their varying professional development needs. Woven into Keisha and her team's work were a number of different data-collection strategies that informed the direction of their teaching as well as the direction their professional development took over the course of a school year. The selection of a focus for professional development (in this case, reading comprehension), the collection of different types of data to inform that focus (e.g., test scores, progress monitoring, student work, observation field notes), and different professional development strategies (e.g., book study, protocols, lesson study, action research) all must intentionally and systematically intersect as those responsible for job-embedded professional development create a *theory of change*.

WHAT IS A THEORY OF CHANGE, WHY DO YOU NEED ONE, AND HOW DO YOU GET ONE?

Now that you have a clearer picture of what job-embedded professional learning would look like in action, and you are armed with the tools to structure job-embedded learning, how do you create your own plan? If you are interested in creating powerful, job-embedded professional development that can really meet the demands of addressing all of the great complexity inherent in teacher learning, it will be important for you to develop and articulate with your school community an explicit *theory of change* that will lead to realizing your teacher-learning goals. A theory of change (Connell & Klem, 2000) is an explicit data-driven plan for achieving long-term professional learning goals by identifying the preconditions and professional development tools necessary to lead to changes in teaching practice and student learning. The theory of change outlines how a school faculty creates a system to initiate and sustain instructional change that strengthens student learning.

In the absence of a theory of change, job-embedded professional development can become an unsystematic piling up of a group of unrelated experiences for teachers as they jump from strategy to strategy and/or collect data here and there without intentionality or purpose. For example, in the illustration previously provided, Keisha might have begun with a book study focused on reading comprehension. Then, when the three-week book study ended, a group member might have found an archived Webinar on self-regulated learning she thought the teachers in her group would enjoy, and this Webinar could have been used at their next meetings. Later that month, Keisha's team might have decided to address the concerns related to their use of the recently purchased smart boards, and so on.

While this nonexample could continue, it is easy to see that there is no thread that ties these teachers' job-embedded, professional learning experiences together, and there is no long-range plan for teacher and student learning. An unsystematic piling up of disconnected and unrelated professional development acts can be just as ineffective as the one-shot deal. Hence, it's important for every educator leading job-embedded professional learning to develop and articulate a theory of change. This theory of change should take into account all of the building blocks of professional learning discussed in Chapter 1 of this text. Additionally, this theory of change must be developed with the team and be flexible enough to be responsive to team members as they identify barriers to their professional learning that must be addressed. We turn to one last illustration to exemplify the concept of theory of change.

ILLUSTRATION: ELEMENTARY SCHOOL TEACHER LEADER KEVIN SMITH

Kevin Smith, a teacher leading professional development in his elementary school through facilitating an inquiry-oriented PLC, began meeting with his colleagues before school opened in August. During the group's early meetings, they engaged in a series of conversations about their struggling students' needs and a series of readings related to engaged instruction. One of the topics that generated much attention from these early group discussions was the role that culturally responsive teaching might play in helping the teachers reach their struggling students.

The group had learned that culturally responsive teaching uses the cultural knowledge, prior experiences, and performance styles of diverse students to make learning more appropriate and effective by teaching to and through the strengths of these students (Gay, 2000). Additionally, the group had come to recognize culturally responsive teaching as multidimensional, including elements of curriculum content, learning context, classroom climate, student-teacher relationships, instructional techniques, and performance assessments. As a result of this shared learning and identification of a shared goal, the group gave birth to the following wonderings: "How do we create more culturally responsive teaching in our classrooms?" and "What happens to student learning when we create more culturally responsive teaching?" The group members connected their work to their school's improvement plan, their district's initiative, and their community's needs.

In mid-October, the group members met to begin developing their inquiry plan. They began their meeting by devoting ten minutes to a protocol called Connections designed to help learning-community members build a bridge from where they are or have been (mentally, physically, etc.) to where they will be going and what they will be doing in the PLC meeting (see the National School Reform Faculty Web site for additional instructions on this protocol: www.harmonyschool.org/nsrf/protocol/index.html).

Once Connections was completed, Kevin began, "We left our last PLC meeting with two questions that we agreed to explore together this year." Kevin pointed to the chart paper he had hung up prior to the start of the meeting that read, "How do we create more culturally responsive teaching in our classrooms? What happens to student learning when we create more culturally responsive teaching?" He knew it would be important to have that question front and center during each of their meetings in order to keep the group's eye on the goal.

He continued,

I think that at today's meeting, it might be beneficial for us to develop a plan for how our inquiry will proceed, but first I need to confirm that we are all comfortable with the decision to pursue this question, and that we are committed to engaging in action research in order to pursue it. The floor is open for thoughts and comments for five minutes.

The group agreed and dialogue ensued reaffirming the membership's commitment toward culturally responsive practices and the action-research process.

At the end of five minutes, Kevin said,

I hear that we all share a passion and commitment to devote our PLC work to the exploration of this question, so let's begin by discussing how we could collect data to that end. Let's brainstorm a list of the information we would need to help us answer this question and then match up data-collection strategies that would help us generate this information. This is a time to be open to all possibilities and not limit our brainstorming in any way; so, let's begin.

Kevin drew a two-column chart on the whiteboard that he filled in as PLC members generated ideas. The group began by generating a list of the types of information that they believed would help them better understand their children and their children's culture, and Kevin listed this information in the left-hand column (see Table 11.1).

When no more new ideas were forthcoming from PLC group members, Kevin stood and admired the chart they had created together. They had created a lengthy list of areas they knew they needed more knowledge about in order to teach these struggling students. Next, Kevin brainstormed with the group the kinds of data that would help them get the information they deemed potentially useful. In the right-hand column of the chart, Kevin scripted their ideas. Table 11.1 represents the chart that was generated by the group.

Although the group seemed pleased with their list, some of them looked overwhelmed at the amount of data that was at hand. As a result, Kevin proceeded to ask the group to carefully evaluate their chart and the data suggestions as he posed the following questions:

- What data-collection strategies that appeared on our list surprised you?
- What data-collection strategies would be great data sources but are impractical to obtain?
- What data sources do you think would be most valuable and why?
- What structures need to be in place to support this data-collection effort?

Table 11.1   Data-Collection Exercise

Shared Inquiry Questions:

How do we create more culturally responsive teaching in our classrooms?

What happens to student learning when we create more culturally responsive teaching?

Information That Would Help Us Answer Our Question	Data-Collection Strategies That Would Generate This Information
Find out more about the neighborhoods our students live in.	Field notes.
Find out what parents expect from the school community.	Survey. Conduct home visits.
Find out how our students are performing in each academic area and subarea.	Assessment data.
Find out what goals students set for themselves.	Student interviews or surveys.
Find out what management patterns are familiar to students. Find out what teachers expect from their students and how they encourage students to meet expectations and recognize their accomplishments.	Focus groups with teachers. Classroom observations.
Get to know students' learning-style preferences.	Survey.
Utilize content and resources that connect to students' backgrounds.	Do a search for books, articles, and Web resources. Journal about new strategies that might benefit your students and why.
Develop a variety of learning activities that are engaging and reflective of students' backgrounds (cooperative learning, literature circles, and community projects).	Do a search for books, articles, and Web resources. Journal about new strategies that might benefit your students and why.
Find out how students respond (in both learning and engagement) to various teaching strategies.	Student-work analysis. Field notes. Student feedback sheets. Journal about changes you are seeing in your teaching and with your students.

Through discussion of these questions, the group committed to collecting and analyzing a variety of data sources to gain insights into their questions. For example, at the beginning of their work together, the group members decided to distribute a survey to both parents and students to better understand their own goals as well as the expectations they had of the school. During the bulk of the year, the group also believed that saving student work samples, tracking student growth on assessments, as well as notes from peer observations would help them make sense of their ability to transfer new ideas about culturally responsive teaching to the classroom. Each of the members also committed to keeping a journal that included field notes as well as personal reflections on their teaching. Finally, they decided that by asking students to complete feedback sheets after engaging in culturally relevant teaching, they would be able to include student voices in the findings.

Kevin continued,

> OK, great, we have a plan for collecting data. Now, we need to establish when and how we are going to do this plan. Our PLC meetings are the first Wednesday of every month. How about if I list our monthly meeting dates on the board, and we can use that to set goals for when this data is collected, not to mention which of us will be involved in collecting it, when we'll do some analysis, and when we'll share what we learned with others. Clearly, some data we will all be collecting, but some data (like the survey data) we should divide and conquer.

Through discussion, the timeline represented in Table 11.2 emerged. As shown, this plan integrated the inquiry process as well as many of the protocols for looking at student work, resolving dilemmas, and generating lesson plans that are offered by the National School Reform Faculty as tools for deepening teaching practice. Additionally, the plan required the learning-community members to do data collection outside of the learning-community meeting times, and the principal of the school was able to allocate this important time for the teachers and Kevin to engage in the professional work associated with the inquiry.

Once their shared question had been formed, their data-collection plan generated, and their timeline created, Kevin asked the group to evaluate their work so far using a set of prompts that help teacher researchers maintain the integrity of their work. These were thoughts that Kevin regularly kept in the back of his mind as he coached, and now he would make those questions explicit to his group:

1. Have we established a connection between the inquiry question and all other components of the inquiry plan (data collection, data analysis, and the timeline)?

2. Are we using multiple forms of data?

Table 11.2   Articulating a Theory of Change

Shared Inquiry Questions:

How do we create more culturally responsive teaching in our classrooms?

What happens to student learning when we create more culturally responsive teaching?

Month	Before Meeting	During Meeting
September	• Read articles on culturally responsive teaching (all members) • Review own student-assessment data	• Connections • Text-based discussion on articles • Establish groups' shared goals and inquiry questions • Reflection
October	• Develop, distribute, and collect parent and student surveys (Jane, Mark, and Beth) • Collect and review baseline-assessment data (each classroom teacher) • Visit neighborhoods (entire PLC; invite pastor)	• Connections • Analyze parent and student surveys using the chalk talk protocol • Engage in a text-based discussion of culturally responsive teaching strategies • Reflection
November	• Student interviews (each teacher completes three interviews) • Peer observation (each teacher observes one other group member) • Collect student work as teacher implements culturally responsive teaching strategies (each teacher) • Take field notes as teacher implements culturally responsive teaching strategies (each teacher)	• Connections • Tuning protocols or dilemma protocols focused on teachers sharing their efforts to engage in culturally responsive teaching strategies (three presenters; four groups) • Analyze student interviews • Reflection

Month	Before Meeting	During Meeting
December	• Read article about culturally responsive teaching strategies (each teacher) • Peer observations (each teacher observes one other group member) • Collect student work • Take field notes as teacher implements culturally responsive teaching strategies (each teacher) • Review student-assessment data (each teacher)	• Connections • Engage in a text-based discussion of culturally responsive teaching strategies • Tuning protocols or dilemma protocols focused on teachers sharing their efforts to engage in culturally responsive teaching strategies (three presenters; four groups) • Reflection
January	• Collect student work • Peer observations (each teacher observes one other group member) • Take field notes as teacher implements culturally responsive teaching strategies (each teacher)	• Connections • Use protocols to analyze student work • Use consultancy to explore dilemmas you are having with your students • Reflection
February	• Collect student work • Peer observations (each teacher observes one other group member) • Take field notes as teacher implements culturally responsive teaching strategies (each teacher)	• Connections • Use protocols to analyze student work • Use consultancy to explore dilemmas you are having with your students • Reflection

(Continued)

Table 11.2 (Continued)

Month	Before Meeting	During Meeting
March	• Collect student-work samples • Take field notes as teacher implements culturally responsive teaching strategies (each teacher) • Review student-assessment data (each teacher) • Meet with Kevin (each teacher met with Kevin or another trained coach in the school to closely examine the individual data that they had collected)	• Connections • Use protocols to analyze student work • Use consultancy to explore dilemmas you are having with your students • Reflection
April	• Repeat survey (Jennifer, Mike, and Angi) • Repeat subset of student interviews • Gather all data • Engage in preliminary analysis by reading through own data	• Connections • Analyze survey data • Analyze data across learning-community meetings to generate overarching findings from the year's inquiry work • Reflection
May	• Develop presentation	• Provide an overview of results to principal • Share at faculty meeting and with district office • Reflection

3. Is our plan doable?

4. Can we make our timeline work for implementing the inquiry plan?

Kevin volunteered to type up their plan, and he ended the PLC meeting with a reminder:

> We have engaged in some hard work today to develop a plan for our inquiry. What we have essentially done is worked together to articulate our theory of change—how we will work together over time to become more culturally responsive teachers and how we will keep track of our progress using data. I'll e-mail the plan to everyone before our next meeting. I will also be keeping a notebook of the artifacts we generate from our inquiry work, but we will each need to keep our own inquiry notebook as well. Just as I will document our collective work, we will each need to document our individual work toward making sense of how culturally responsive teaching is working for ourselves and our students.
>
> We also want to remember that even though we commit a plan to paper, it's OK for us to deviate from our plan as our professional development unfolds. We may discover something along the way in our data that leads us in a new direction. The final part of the theory of change we articulated today is planning and identifying what we will use to measure progress along the way. Our data will help us do this as well as chart new directions in our plan when the data calls for one. We can help each other remain open to shifts in our plan along the way by periodically returning to it and suggesting modifications based on what we are learning from our data. We need to remember that the plan we constructed today is important to provide direction, but it isn't set in stone! Let's spend our last five minutes writing a reflection on today's meeting.

PLC group members took out a piece of paper and jotted down their feelings and thoughts about the ways the day's meeting had transpired.

This illustration indicates one way staff developers can facilitate the articulation of a theory of change. Note that Kevin attended to the building blocks of professional learning discussed in the first part of this book and, in this example, collaboratively led the teachers in finding a focus for their professional development endeavors during the school year as well as the forms of data they would use to keep track of their progress along the way (surveys, student work, assessments, notes from peer observations, and journals) and the job-embedded, professional development strategies that created the context for their work (literature study, professional learning communities, action research, and protocols).

TIPS FOR MAKING THE PERFECT MATCH FOR PROFESSIONAL LEARNING

In Part I of this text, we noted that teacher professional learning is an inherently incredibly complex endeavor. As you end this chapter, you can begin to truly understand this statement. Looking back across the preceding chapters, we've discussed the many building blocks of powerful professional learning, how to help teachers and principals reconceptualize their roles, how to find time and resources to make job-embedded professional development a reality, and we've become familiar with the many different job-embedded, professional development strategies discussed in Part II. As if that weren't enough, the person developing and leading job-embedded learning in a school or district must also align building blocks, role reconfigurations, time, resources, and strategies to perfectly match professional development efforts to teacher and student learning goals. Because the concept of matching is so complex, and so critical to leading job-embedded learning, we end this chapter with five tips to help you make perfect matches!

Tip 1: Develop a Large Toolbox of Job-Embedded, Professional Learning Strategies

One might think that after reading a variety of books, you have knowledge of all the wonderful professional development tools available to teachers. Our experience is that new research-based approaches to job-embedded professional development are constantly emerging. Thus, continually engaging in ongoing professional development for yourself by attending national conferences, like the National Staff Development Council and other professional development organizations, will keep your knowledge fresh. You might consider purchasing a subscription to the *Journal of Staff Development* and regularly scan professional libraries or publishers' catalogues for publications of new professional development tools. Remember, just as we engage in life-long learning to enhance student learning, keeping abreast of new professional development innovations is equally as important to our growth.

Tip 2: Cultivate a Clear Understanding of and Access to Data

The word *data* enters our conversations regularly in today's era of accountability. We are more comfortable today than ever before using student-learning data to inform instruction. The problem is that we haven't always used student-learning data to inform our professional development efforts. Data and professional development must go hand in hand as we create our theory of change. Data allows us to identify hidden patterns; and by sharing this data with teachers who have influence on charting their own professional development, they become empowered to transform this data into information that guides their professional development choices and, ultimately, their instructional decision making. Job-embedded professional development relies on data-informed decision making. The use and analysis of student data to inform professional development planning requires regular data collection and ongoing implementation of planned, focused professional development.

Tip 3: Gauge the Readiness of
Your Colleagues for Collaboration and
Match the Tool to Their Level of Readiness

A variety of preconditions need to exist in order for your team to engage in job-embedded, professional development work. First, your team must be motivated to commit the time and energy to do the work. Second, a team must collectively acknowledge that we improve when we make time for reflection. This means we sometimes have to slow down even when we feel rushed to meet the demands of the daily routine. Third, we must create relationships among ourselves that are safe and open to critical feedback. We must be able to ask each other hard questions. This is easier when we focus on the work rather than on ourselves. Fourth, everyone must be willing to change his or her teaching. Collaboration requires building and using new knowledge together. Fifth, the team members will benefit by developing shared structures for their conversations. These structures should encourage collaboration and create parity and equity within the group. Finally, collaboration will require a sense of camaraderie, support, and celebration that keeps the learning spirit going even through tough times.

Tip 4: Match the Tool to the Available Time,
or Create the Available Time to Match the Tool

Unfortunately, McDiarmid (1995) notes that the increasing demands posed by both daily teaching and reform consume the bulk of teachers' energy and attention. We need to rally together as a profession to redefine professional development as a central part of teaching and move most professional development decisions to the school level so that they can be embedded in teachers' daily work. Some reformers have actually recommended that, like our international colleagues, we need to devote at least 20 percent of teachers' work time to professional study and collaborative work. Although that may not be attainable in our current context, we need to begin thinking outside the box to work inside the clock and reshape teacher working conditions, so teachers will have the support required to plan and implement today's ambitious reform efforts.

As discussed in Chapter 3, there are many ways to carve out time within the school day for teachers to learn collaboratively. However, we also need to be advocates beyond our school buildings and actively educate others about the importance of providing teachers with time to learn within their school day. Some activities you might consider engaging in include creating a statewide network to garner support from the public and policymakers; meeting with businesses, community groups, and parent organizations to explain the importance of job-embedded professional learning; inviting school-board and central-office administrators to watch your professional learning in action; and being sure that your theory of change clearly links school- and individual-improvement goals with the time created for professional development.

Tip 5: Take the Time to Plan and to Monitor Your Plan

Whether you are planning your diet, your retirement, your career path, or your daily lesson plans, planning promotes success. We plan for lots of other things in our lives, so why not intentionally and systematically plan how we use our professional development resources so that they have the greatest chance of making an impact on student learning? There's really no good reason not to. Planning simply involves organizing and preparing ahead of time and making adjustments along the way when necessary. It means monitoring your situation throughout the year; and in doing so, you can tailor your resources to your school's learning needs. By creating a clear plan or theory of action and monitoring your plan along the way, your professional development activities will lead to authentic changes in teacher and student learning.

CONCLUDING THOUGHTS

This chapter helps us think about how to cultivate the skills needed to plan powerful professional development once we have acquired the tools that support job-embedded learning. We now complete our professional journey by exploring some important lessons learned by educators experienced in planning effective professional learning opportunities.

12

Effective Professional Development Within Your School Walls

Lessons Learned

I never teach my pupils; I only attempt to provide the conditions in which they can learn.

—Albert Einstein

Anyone who stops learning is old, whether at twenty or eighty.

—Henry Ford

The opening quotes to this chapter embody what job-embedded professional development is all about—creating the conditions for teachers to learn throughout their professional lifetimes and, in the process, keeping teachers vibrant and alive in their teaching! The purpose of this book is to explore everything that is needed to create these conditions. To review, in Part I of this book, we deeply examined the critical elements to consider when planning job-embedded professional development. In Part II, we explored tools that can facilitate job-embedded professional development, and we identified the unique contribution each tool can make to facilitate changes in teaching practice. In Part III, we examined the details associated with selecting the right tools at the right time to address the professional development needs of your school or district.

In this last chapter, we draw upon the expertise of principals, teacher leaders, and district- and state-level educators who have paved the way for others to follow in the area of job-embedded professional development, offering ten lessons about job-embedded professional development learned from their experiences. Although each of these educators are important to supporting the work of job-embedded professional development, it is really the teachers and teacher leaders who can make authentic learning occur within their school and classroom walls. Becoming a teacher leader armed with a strong set of professional learning tools shows promise for transforming the future of the teaching profession.

In addition to lessons learned from educators within the United States, we can also benefit from exploring international perspectives in job-embedded professional development. For example, in reviewing the McKinsey Report (2007), we find that job-embedded professional development is the norm in countries with high student performance. Specifically, the report indicates that, in Finland and Japan, student learning is greatly enhanced by creating school cultures that enable teachers to learn from each other. In these schools, children are increasingly successful because of the teachers' collaboration. They plan, observe, and support each other's development as a part of their professional responsibilities. This collaborative culture allows teachers to continuously learn. The learning culture in Japan's schools is built around the lesson study tool we explored in Part II of the book. As teachers work together to plan, observe, and refine individual lessons, they strengthen student learning related to specific learning objectives. As you can imagine, the culture of the Japanese schools is to make sure that best practices are shared throughout the school. According to the McKinsey Report (2007), "When a brilliant American teacher retires, almost all of the lesson plans and practices that she has developed also retire. When a Japanese teacher retires, she leaves a legacy" (p. 34).

The McKinsey Report also provides heightened levels of student learning in the Boston schools as well. Using creative scheduling, the schools provide common planning time for teachers who teach the same subjects at the same grade level. During this time, the teachers jointly plan and revise teaching practices in light of student-assessment data. They also use peer observation to share and cultivate successful teaching practices. In combination, these tools create a collaborative learning culture within Boston's schools.

TEN LESSONS FOR MAKING JOB-EMBEDDED PROFESSIONAL DEVELOPMENT A SUCCESS AT YOUR SCHOOL

By standing on the shoulders of others, both within and outside the United States, who have charted the path before us, we can jump-start our own ability to lead within our schools. To these ends, we briefly share ten lessons learned from watching these professional development trailblazers, the innovative leaders in our field.

Lesson 1: Use Data at Every Stage

As you create opportunities for job-embedded professional learning within your school, make data a centerpiece. By making data a centerpiece of your professional conversations, you will create a collaborative culture of professional learning driven by data-based decision making. You will use data to plan professional development activities. Teachers will begin recognizing the power of attending to multiple sources of data to better understand their students' needs. By attending to these multiple sources of data, teachers focus on learning how to better meet the needs of their students, and as teachers begin to focus on their students and see their different needs, a sense of urgency develops serving as a catalyst for action that motivates professional learning. Finally, the most sophisticated act of using data as a part of job-embedded professional development is using data in a way that leads to changes in professional practice.

Lesson 2: Share Your Findings Widely, and Celebrate Your Successes

Engaging in change can be exhausting and invigorating at the same time. The trick is to keep teachers teetering back in forth between the two feelings. One way to do this is to be sure to both share your findings widely and celebrate your successes, even the small ones. By creating a culture that embraces the act of making learning public, teachers will be provided the opportunity to not only learn from each other but feel like they are contributing to their colleagues' learning as well. Remember the lesson we learned from our Japanese neighbors: "When a brilliant American teacher retires, almost all of the lesson plans and practices that she has developed also retire. When a Japanese teacher retires, she leaves a legacy" (McKinsey Report, 2007, p. 34). By sharing and celebrating our learning, we too can leave a legacy!

Lesson 3: Build the Back Porch by
Providing the Necessary Resources for Success!

We agree with the saying, "If you don't invest, you can't expect the best!" Building the back porch requires investing in our teaching force to assure our students' success. We also agree that when we moved away from the one-room schoolhouse in America, we forgot to build the back porch. The back-porch metaphor represents a place for teachers to share and reflect collaboratively as they create knowledge *for, in,* and *of* practice. In Part I of the book, we illustrate the key components of professional learning that have been missing in schools. We also identify ways that you can carve out the necessary time and resources to make professional learning happen. This will require thinking outside of the box about how we can use our existing resources as well as how we can garner new resources to support our goals.

Lesson 4: Systematically Draw Upon
All Three Sources of Professional Knowledge

Probably, the most important lesson that underpins the movement toward job-embedded professional development is the importance of providing teachers support in creating all three types of professional knowledge. This requires systematically and intentionally planning for the development of knowledge *for, in,* and *of* practice related to the school-improvement effort that your team is facing. These sources of knowledge help construct each of the other professional knowledge building blocks introduced in Part I. This also means that those leading professional development efforts need to help their colleagues as well as their administrators understand why all three knowledge sources will lead to changes in student performance and in school culture. By using the planning tools in this book, you can jump-start your success!

Lesson 5: Develop Job-Embedded Expertise
Within Your School Building by Nurturing
the Development of Other Teacher Leaders

One of the biggest mistakes school leaders, both teacher leaders and administrators, can make is neglecting to nurture the development of new teacher leaders who have the ability to facilitate job-embedded professional development. Given the attrition and turnover of faculty in schools, as well as impending retirements across the county, we cannot assume that those who are leading our schools today will remain in the schools tomorrow. That said, your students will benefit each year that you cultivate new leadership, build deeper professional knowledge bases, and expand teacher roles. The professional learning culture cannot be about a single person or leader. By spreading the knowledge and making professional learning a part of every teacher's work in your school, you begin to institutionalize the activity in a way that can survive changes in leadership.

Lesson 6: Align to School, County, and State Goals

Given the intensity of teachers' daily work, as we engage in professional development we need to be cognizant of the multiple and complex expectations that demand their attention. The challenge is to help teachers find ways to align their self-identified, professional development needs with school, county, and state goals. The more alignment that can be drawn, the easier it will be for teachers to hit the multiple targets they are expected to accomplish. Although alignment is a great approach to meeting multiple expectations, sometimes school, district, and state leadership roll out so many expectations that no one could possibly realize the magnitude of changes requested at one time. In these cases, you will need to take an advocacy position that helps those in decision-making positions understand that more is not always better. They need to understand what it will take to hit the bull's-eye. They need to learn that alignment and a manageable number of initiatives can actually lead to a bull's-eye—a bull's-eye that represents real change in student learning.

Lesson 7: Make Professional Learning a Part of, Rather Than Apart From, the Daily Work of Teachers

Making professional learning *a part of* rather than *apart from* the daily work of teachers requires preparing teachers to make the shift from traditional to job-embedded professional development. Although this idea may seem like a message that would be welcomed by educators, the movement represents a paradigm shift. Remember the old adage that if Rip Van Winkle returned after being asleep for one hundred years the easiest institutions for him to identify would be churches and schools? Many schools today really don't look that much different than one hundred years ago. This is the same for professional development. Even in spite of a century of research indicating the importance of cultivating an inquiry stance in teachers and providing on-the-job learning opportunities, professional development has remained a "sit and get" activity. Professional learning will only become a part of our daily work when job-embedded professional development becomes the norm and teachers embrace professional learning as a part of each and every school day. You can begin making professional learning a part of your school's culture by creating a back porch for collaboration and introducing professional learning tools that are powerful enough to influence student learning.

Lesson 8: Communicate Honestly and Regularly

Communication among teachers in your school is a key to job-embedded professional development. The goal is to create an environment where teachers feel comfortable sharing their dilemmas with each other, asking hard questions of each other, and creating new knowledge by reflecting together. To do this, teachers must create trust and a repertoire of communication skills that reflect critical friendship rather than mere criticism. In collaborative professional development contexts, *critical* means raising important, key, essential, or urgent questions about the topic being explored. It is important to spend time discussing and developing communication norms about how to give feedback and how to question in a sensitive manner.

Additionally, communication with those outside your immediate learning group must also be effective and regular. When we fail to communicate with those who have the power to support our collaborative work, we can cause a good professional development plan to fail. When we communicate our professional development efforts and processes effectively, we are able to increase support, decrease resistance, and encourage effective and positive movement through the change process.

Lesson 9: Match Your Expectations for Job-Embedded Professional Development to the Amount of Time, Resources, and Energy You Can Realistically Devote to It

Confronted with the need to trim budgets, it is easy for schools and districts to gravitate toward job-embedded professional development because they think it is cost free. "No longer will we have to hire expensive outside consultants, and we can just rely on the people we already pay to lead professional development efforts," is a misconceived notion about job-embedded professional learning. While job-embedded PD can save money, it is not cost free. It is important to reflect on the third chapter in this book to figure out ways you can create the time and find the money necessary to support learning within the four walls of your school. You cannot expect job-embedded learning to thrive if you do not invest time and resources into creating the conditions for everyday teachers' learning to flourish. As you invest time and resources, remember that while job-embedded professional learning is not cost free, it is more cost effective! It is clear that you will yield a much higher return rate on investments you make in this form of professional development than in the one-shot deal alone (Desimone, 2009).

Lesson 10: Remember, Real Change Takes Pressure Paired With Support

The most important lesson we have learned about teacher professional learning is that pressure to learn must be paired with support. Michael

Fullan (1991) explains that change in instruction depends on what teachers do and think, but that teachers are actually quite amenable to a mix of pressures and supports. Fullan notes, "Successful change projects always include elements of both pressure and support. Pressure without support leads to resistance and alienation; support without pressure leads to drift or waste of resources" (p. 91). Similarly, we view the relationship between pressure and support much like a balance or scale. The amount of pressure placed on a teacher must be paired with an equal amount of support for the learning. This book was designed to help you think about how to provide the important supports our teachers—and more importantly, our students—deserve.

PARTING COMMENTS

Your school's journey toward making teacher learning a part of rather than apart from their daily work will be greatly facilitated by using these and other job-embedded, professional development tools. We believe your efforts are critically important to helping teachers, students, and schools thrive! Roland Barth (1981) makes the case for teacher learning the best when he says,

> Nothing within a school has more impact upon students in terms of skills development, self-confidence, or classroom behavior than the personal and professional growth of their teachers. When teachers examine, question, reflect on their ideas and develop new practices that lead towards their ideals, students are alive. When teachers stop growing, so do their students. (p. 145)

These comments, written almost three decades ago, still ring true today. Your challenge is to breathe renewed life and energy into our teaching force by finding ways to create job-embedded learning opportunities that become a part of each day they teach. For today's teachers and the children whom they teach, there is no work that is more important!

References and Additional Reading

Allen, D. W., & Le Blanc, A. C. (2005). *Collaborative peer coaching that improves instruction.* Thousand Oaks, CA: Corwin.

Badiali, B., & Hammond, D. J. (2005). Co-teaching as an alternative to the "take-over" phenomenon. *Pennsylvania Teacher Educator, 4,* 32–41.

Ball, D. L., & McDiarmid, G. W. (1989). *The subject matter preparation of teachers* (Issue Paper 89–4). E. Lansing, MI: National Center of Research on Teacher Learning, Michigan State University.

Banilower, E. R., & Shimkus, E. S. (2004). *Professional development observation study.* Chapel Hill, NC: Horizon Research.

Barth, R. S. (1981). The principal as staff developer. *Journal of Education, 163*(2), 144–162.

Barth, R. S. (1990). *Improving schools from within: Teachers, parents, and principals can make the difference.* San Francisco: Jossey-Bass.

Barth, R. S. (2001a). *Learning by heart.* San Francisco: Jossey-Bass,

Barth, R. S. (2001b). Principal centered professional development. *Theory Into Practice, 25*(3), 156–160.

Becker, J. M. (n.d.). *Peer coaching for improvement of teaching and learning.* Retrieved December 6, 2009, from http://www.teachnet.org/TNPI/research/growth/becker.htm.

Bolman, L. G., & Deal, T. E. (1994). *Becoming a teacher leader: From isolation to collaboration.* Thousand Oaks, CA: Corwin.

Borko, H. (2004). Professional development and teacher learning: Mapping the terrain. *Educational Researcher, 33*(8), 3–15.

Borthwick, A., & Pierson, M. (Eds.). (2008). *Transforming classroom practice: Professional development strategies.* Eugene, OR: International Society for Technology in Education.

Buehl, D. (2001). *Classroom strategies for interactive learning.* Washington, DC: International Reading Association.

Bullough, R. V., Jr., & Gitlin, A. (1995). *Becoming a student of teaching: Methodologies for exploring self and school context.* New York: Garland.

Caro-Bruce, C., Flessner, R., Klehr, M., & Zeichner, K. (2007). *Creating equitable classrooms through action research.* Thousand Oaks, CA: Corwin.

Childs-Bowen, D., Moller, G., & Scrivner, J. (2000). Principals: Leaders of leaders. *NASSP Bulletin, 84*(616), 27–34.

Clauset, K. H., Lick, D. W., & Murphey, C. U. (2009). *Schoolwide action research for professional learning communities: Improving student learning through the whole-faculty study groups approach.* Thousand Oaks, CA: Corwin.

Cochran-Smith, M., & Lytle, S. L. (1993). *Inside/outside: Teacher research and knowledge.* New York: Teachers College Press.

Cochran-Smith, M., & Lytle, S. L. (1999). Relationships of knowledge and practice: Teacher learning in communities. *Review of Research in Education, 24,* 249–305.

Cochran-Smith, M., & Lytle, S. L. (2001). Beyond certainty: Taking an inquiry stance on practice. In A. Lieberman & L. Miller (Eds.), *Teachers caught in the action: Professional development that matters* (pp. 45–58). New York: Teachers College Press.

Cochran-Smith, M., & Lytle, S. L. (2009) *Inquiry as stance: Practitioner research for the next generation.* New York: Teachers College Press.

Cohen, D. K. (1990). A revolution in one classroom: The case of Mrs. Oublier. *Educational Evaluation and Policy, 12,* 311–325.

Co-Intelligence Institute. (2003–2008). *Open space technology.* Retrieved December 3, 2009, from http://www.co-intelligence.org/P-Openspace.html.

Conderman, G., Vresnahan, V., & Pedersen, T. (2008). *Purposeful co-teaching: Real cases and effective strategies.* Thousand Oaks, CA: Corwin.

Connell, J. P., & Klem, A. M. (2000). You can get there from here: Using a theory of change approach to plan urban education reform. *Journal of Educational and Psychological Consultation, 11,* 93–120.

Conservapedia. (2009). *Norman Vincent Peale quotes.* Retrieved December 3, 2009, from http://www.conservapedia.com/Norman_Vincent_Peale.

Corwin. (2008). *Mentoring, coaching, and collaboration.* Thousand Oaks, CA: Author.

Crowther, F. (2009). *Developing teacher leaders: How teacher leadership enhances school success.* Thousand Oaks, CA: Corwin.

Dana, N. F. (2009). *Leading with passion and knowledge: The principal as action researcher.* Thousand Oaks, CA: Corwin.

Dana, N. F., & Yendol-Hoppey, D. (2008). *The reflective educator's guide to professional development: Coaching inquiry-oriented learning communities.* Thousand Oaks, CA: Corwin.

Dana, N. F., & Yendol-Hoppey, D. (2009). *The reflective educator's guide to classroom research: Learning to teach and teaching to learn through practitioner inquiry* (2nd ed.). Thousand Oaks, CA: Corwin.

Danielson, C. (2006). *Teacher leadership that strengthens professional practice.* Alexandria, VA: Association for Supervision and Curriculum Development.

Darling-Hammond, L. (1987). Schools for tomorrow's teachers. *Teachers College Record 88:* 354–58.

Darling-Hammond, L. (1997a). *Doing what matters most: Investing in quality teaching.* New York: National Commission on Teaching and America's Future.

Darling-Hammond, L. (1997b). *The right to learn: A blueprint for creating schools that work.* San Francisco: Jossey-Bass.

Darling-Hammond, L. (1999). *Teacher quality and student achievement: A review of state policy evidence.* Seattle, WA: Center for the Study of Teaching and Policy.

Davis, M. R. (2009, March 13). *Online professional development weighed as cost-saving tactic.* Retrieved December 3, 2009, from http://www.edweek.org/dd/articles/2009/03/13/04ddprofdev.h02.html.

Dede, C. (2006). *Online professional development for teachers: Emerging models and methods.* Cambridge, MA: Harvard Educational Press.

Desimone, L. M. (2009). Improving impact studies of teachers' professional development: Toward better conceptualizations and measures. *Educational Researcher, 38,* 181–199.

Dewey, J. (1933). *How we think. A restatement of the relation of reflective thinking to the educative process* (Rev. ed.). Boston: D. C. Heath.

DuFour, R. (2004). What is a professional learning community? *Educational Leadership, 61*(8), 6–11.

Easton, L. (2008). *Powerful designs for professional learning.* Oxford, OH: National Staff Development Council.

Elmore, R. (2002). *Bridging the gap between standards and achievement.* Washington, DC: The Albert Shanker Institute.

Feiman-Nemser, S. (2001). From preparation to practice: Designing a continuum to strengthen and sustain teaching. *Teachers College Record 103,* 1013–1055.

Friend, M., & Cook, L. (2003). *Interactions: Coprofessionals* (4th ed.). Boston: Allyn and Bacon.

Fullan, M. (1991). *The new meaning of educational change.* New York: Teachers College Press.

Fullan, M. (2001a). *Leading in a culture of change.* San Francisco: Jossey-Bass.

Fullan, M. (2001b). *The new meaning of educational change* (3rd ed.). New York: Teachers College Press.

Gay, G. (2000). *Culturally responsive teaching: Theory, research, & practice.* New York: Teachers College Press.

Grossman, P. L. (1990). *The making of a teacher: Teacher knowledge and teacher education.* New York: Teachers College Press.

Hord, S. M. (1997). *Professional learning communities: Communities of continuous inquiry and improvement.* Austin, TX: Southwest Educational Development Laboratory.

Hubbell, D. (2005, April 23). *Focus on fractured fairy tales and fluency flourishes.* Presentation at the Teaching, Inquiry, and Innovation Showcase, Gainesville, Fl.

Jacobs, J. L. (2007, February 24). *Coaching for equity: Meeting the needs of diverse learners through field supervision.* Paper presented at the annual meeting of the American Association of Colleges for Teacher Education, New York. Retrieved December 6, 2009, from http://www.allacademic.com/meta/p142691_index.html.

Jay, A. B., & Stong, M. W. (2008). *A guide to literacy coaching: Helping teachers increase student achievement.* Thousand Oaks, CA: Corwin.

Johnston, J., Knight, M., & Miller, L. (2007). Finding time for teams. *Journal of Staff Development, 28*(2), 14–18.

Jolly, A., & Dana, N. F. (2009). Creating and managing powerful professional learning teams. *Edweek.org.* Retrieved July 16, 2009, from http://event.on24.com/eventRegistration/EventLobbyServlet?target=lobby.jsp&eventid=142361&sessionid=1&key=B78B2CF08A60EB62A1194FAC7A42C7F5&eventuserid=24604697.

Joyce, B. R., & Showers, B. (1983). *Power in staff development through research on training.* Alexandria, VA: Association of Supervision and Curriculum Development.

Joyce, B. R., & Showers, B. (1995). *Student achievement through staff development.* White Plains, NY: Longman, Inc.

Katzenmeyer, M., & Moller, G. (1996). *Awakening the sleeping giant: Leadership development for teachers.* Thousand Oaks, CA: Corwin.

Keller, B. (2008). Hitting the books. *Education Week, 02*(01), 4, 6. Retrieved December 30, 2009, from http://www.edweek.org/tsb/articles/2008/09/10/01books.h02.html.

Khorsheed, K. (2007). Four places to dig deep to find more time for teacher collaboration. *Journal of Staff Development, 28*(2), 43–45.

Killion, J., & Harrison, C. (2006). *Taking the lead: New roles for teachers and school-based coaches.* Oxford, OH: National Staff Development Council.

Knight, J. (2007). *Instructional coaching: A partnership approach to improving instruction.* Thousand Oaks, CA: Corwin.

Knight, J. (2009). *Coaching: Approaches and perspectives.* Thousand Oaks, CA: Corwin.

Lambert, L. (1998). *Building leadership capacity in schools.* Alexandria, VA: Association for Supervision and Curriculum Development.

Lambert, L. (2000). Framing reform for the new millennium: Leadership capacity in schools and districts. *CJEAP, 14.* Retrieved December 11, 2009, from http://www.umanitoba.ca/publications/cjeap/articles/lambert.html.

Lewis, C., Perry, R., & Hurd, J. (2004). A deeper look at lesson study. *Educational Leadership, 61*(5), 18.

Lieberman, A. (1995a). Practices that support teacher development: Transforming conceptions of professional learning. *Phi Delta Kappan 76*(8), 591–596.

Lieberman, A. (1995b). *The work of restructuring schools: Building from the ground up.* New York: Teachers College Press.

Lieberman, A., & Miller, L. (1990a). Restructuring schools: What matters and what works. *Phi Delta Kappan, 71*(10), 759–764.

Lieberman, A., & Miller, L. (1990b). Teacher development in professional practice schools. *Teachers College Record, 92,* 105–122.

Lieberman, A., & Miller, L. (1999). *Teachers: Transforming their world and work* (2nd ed.). New York: Teachers College Press.

Lieberman, A., & Miller, L. (2004). *Teacher leadership.* San Francisco, CA: Jossey-Bass.

Lindsey, D. B., Martinez, R. S., & Lindsey, R. B. (2007). *Culturally proficient coaching: Supporting educators to create equitable schools.* Thousand Oaks, CA: Corwin.

Magnusson, S., Krajcik, J., & Borko, H. (1999). Nature, sources, and development of pedagogical content knowledge for science teaching. In J. Gess-Newsome & N. G. Lederman (Eds.), *PCK and science education* (pp. 95–132). Boston: Kluwer Academic Publishers.

Marzano, R., Pickering, D., & Pollock, J. (2001.) *Classroom instruction that works: Research-based strategies for increasing student achievement.* Alexandria, VA: McCrel.

McDiarmid, G. (1995). *Realizing new learning for all students: A framework for the professional development of Kentucky teachers.* East Lansing, MI: Michigan State University, National Center for Research on Teacher Learning.

McDonald, J. P., Mohr, N., Dichter, A., & McDonald, E. C. (2003). *The power of protocols: An educator's guide to better practice.* New York: Teachers College Press.

McKinsey Report. (2007, May). *How the world's best performing school systems come out on top.* Washington, DC: McKinsey & Company.

Morse, A. (2009). *Cultivating a math coaching practice: A guide for K–8 math educators.* Thousand Oaks, CA: Corwin.

National Staff Development Council. (2009, May 16). *Professional development.* Retrieved June 12, 2009, from http://www.nsdc.org/standfor/definition.cfm.

Owen, H. (1997). *Open space technology: A user's guide.* San Francisco: Berrett-Koehler.

Pellicer, I. O., & Anderson, L. W. (1995). *A handbook for teacher leaders.* Thousand Oaks, CA: Corwin.

Poetter, T. S., & Badiali, B. J. (2001). *Teacher leader.* Larchmont, NY: Eye on Education.

Rebora, A. (2009). *Reinventing professional development in tough times.* Retrieved March 16, 2009, from http://www.teachermagazin.org/tsb/articles/2009/03/16/02pd_budget.

Richardson, W. (2006). *Blogs, wikis, podcasts, and other powerful Web tools for classrooms.* Thousand Oaks, CA: Corwin.

Richardson, W. (2010). *Blogs, wikis, podcasts, and other powerful Web tools for classrooms: A multimedia kit for professional development* (3rd ed.). Thousand Oaks, CA: Corwin.

Roberts, S. M., & Pruitt, E. Z. (2009). *Schools as professional learning communities: Collaborative activities and strategies for professional development* (2nd ed.). Thousand Oaks, CA: Corwin.

Roth, W.- M., Masciotra, D., & Boyd, N. (1999). Becoming-in-the-classroom: A case study of teacher development through co-teaching. *Teaching and Teacher Education, 15,* 771–784.

Schön, D. (1983) *The reflective practitioner: How professionals think in action.* London: Temple Smith.

School Improvement Network. (2009). *PD 360.* Retrieved December 11, 2009, from http://www.schoolimprovement.com/pd360-info.cfm.

School Leadership for the 21st Century Initiative. (2001). *Leadership for student learning: Redefining the teacher as leader.* A Report of the Task Force on Teacher Leadership. Washington, DC: Institution for Educational Leadership.

SEDL. (1997). Professional learning communities: What are they and why are they important? *Issues . . . about change, 6*(1). Retrieved December 7, 2009, from http://www.sedl.org/change/issues/issues61.html.

Sergiovanni, T. J. (2000). *The lifeworld of leadership: Creating culture, community, and personal meaning in our schools.* San Francisco: Jossey-Bass.

Sergiovanni, T. J., & Starrat, R. J. (2002). *Supervision: A redefinition.* Boston: McGraw-Hill.

Showers, B. (1985). Teachers coaching teachers. *Educational Leadership, 42*(7): 43–48.

Showers, B., & Joyce, B. (1995). *Student achievement through staff development: Fundamentals of school renewal.* White Plains, NY: Longman.

Shulman, L. S. (1987a, Spring). Knowledge and teaching: Foundations of the new reform. *Harvard Educational Review,* 1–22.

Shulman, L. S. (1987b). The wisdom of practice: Managing complexity in medicine and teaching. In D. C. Berliner & B. V. Rosenshire (Eds.), *Talks to teachers: A festschrift for N. L. Gage* (pp. 369–384). New York: Random House.

Silva, D. Y., Gimbert, B., & Nolan, J. F. (2000). Sliding the doors: Locking and unlocking the possibilities for teacher leadership. *Teachers College Record, 102,* 779–804.

Singleton, G. E., & Linton, C. (2005). *Courageous conversations about race: A field guide for achieving equity in schools.* Thousand Oaks, CA: Corwin.

Sparks, D. (1994). A paradigm shift in staff development. *Journal of Staff Development, 15*(4), 26–29.

Sparks, D. (1997). A new vision for staff development. *Principal, 77,* 20–22.

Sparks, D., & Hirsh, S. (1997). *A new vision for staff development.* Alexandria, VA: Association for Supervision and Curriculum Development.

Sparks, D., & Loucks-Horsley, S. (1990). Five models of teacher development. *Journal of Staff Development, 10*(4), 40–57.

Spillane, J. P. (2008). Distributed leadership. In J. H. Munro (Ed.), *Roundtable viewpoints: Educational leadership* (pp. 36–42). New York: McGraw-Hill.

Stepanek, J., Appel, G., Leong, M., Mangan, M. T., & Mitchell, M. (2007). *Leading lesson study: A practical guide for teachers and facilitators.* Thousand Oaks, CA: Corwin.

Tobin, K., Roth. W.-M., & Zimmerman, A. (2001). Learning to teach science in urban schools. *Journal of Research in Science Teaching, 38,* 941–964.

Tomlinson, C. A. (1999). *The differentiated classroom: Responding to the needs of all learners.* Upper Saddle River, NJ: Prentice Hall.

Valentine, J. (2009). *Instructional practice inventory.* Columbia, MO: Missouri University College of Education. Retrieved December 7, 2009, from http://education.missouri.edu/orgs/mllc/4A_ipi_overview.php.

Villa, R. A., Thousand, J. S., & Nevin, A. I. (2008). *A guide to co-teaching: A multimedia kit for professional development* (2nd ed.). Thousand Oaks, CA: Corwin.

von Frank, V. (2008). *Finding time for professional learning.* Oxford, OH: National Staff Development Council.

Waldron, N., & McLeskey, J. (1998). The effects of inclusive school programs on students with mild and severe learning disabilities. *Exceptional Children, 64,* 395–406.

Wasley, P. A. (1991). *Teachers who lead: The rhetoric of reform and the realities of practice.* New York: Teachers College Press.

Wasley, P. A. (1992). Working together: Teacher leadership and collaboration. In C. Livingston (Ed.), *Teacher leaders: Evolving roles* (pp. 21–55). Washington, DC: National Education Association.

Wasley, P., Hampel, R., & Clark, R. (1997). The puzzle of whole-school change. *Phi Delta Kappan, 78*(9), 690–697.

West, L. (2002). *Content-focused coaching: Transforming mathematics lessons.* Thousand Oaks, CA: Corwin.

Whitaker, T. (2003). *What great principals do differently: Fifteen things that matter most.* Larchmont, NY: Eye on Education.

Whitford, B. L., & Wood, D. (Eds.). (in press). *Teachers learning in community: Realities and possibilities.* Albany: State University of New York Press.

Wood, F. H., & Killian, J., E. (1998). Job-embedded learning makes the difference in school improvement. *Journal of Staff Development, 19*(2), 52–54.

Wood, F. H., & McQuarrie, F., Jr. (1999). On-the-job learning. *Journal of Staff Development, 20*(3), 20–22.

Yendol-Hoppey, D., & Dana, N. F. (2007). *The reflective educator's guide to mentoring: Strengthening practice through knowledge, story, and metaphor.* Thousand Oaks, CA: Corwin.

York-Barr, J., & Duke, K. (2004). What do we know about teacher leadership? Findings from two decades of scholarship. *Review of Educational Research 74,* 255–316.

York-Barr, J., Sommerness, J., & Hur, J. (2008). Teacher leadership. In T. L. Good (Ed.), *21st century education: A reference handbook* (pp. 12–20). Thousand Oaks, CA: Sage.

Index

CORWIN

A SAGE Company

The Corwin logo—a raven striding across an open book—represents the union of courage and learning. Corwin is committed to improving education for all learners by publishing books and other professional development resources for those serving the field of PreK–12 education. By providing practical, hands-on materials, Corwin continues to carry out the promise of its motto: **"Helping Educators Do Their Work Better."**